Peterson, Roy, 1936-
Drawn & quartered : the Trudeau years / cartoons by Roy Peterson ; introductions by Peter C. Newman. Toronto : Key Porter Books, c1984.
192 p. : ill.

1. Trudeau, Pierre Elliott, 1919- - Cartoons, satire, etc.
(Continued on next card)
0919493424 pb 221685X NLC

Drawn & Quartered

THE TRUDEAU YEARS

Cartoons by

Roy Peterson

Introductions by

Peter C. Newman

KEY PORTER BOOKS

Canadian Cataloguing in Publication Data

Peterson, Roy, 1936
 Drawn and quartered

ISBN 0-919493-42-4

1. Canada – Politics and government – 1963 – Anecdotes, facetiae, satire, etc.* 2. Canada – Politics and government – 1963 – Caricatures and cartoons.* I. Trudeau, Pierre Elliott, 1919– Cartoons, satire, etc. II. Newman, Peter C., 1929– III. Title.

FC626.T78P48 1984 971.064'4'0924 C84-098820-6
F1034.3.P48 1984

Key Porter Books
70 The Esplanade
Toronto, Ontario
Canada M5E 1R2

Design: Joanna Gertler
Cover Art: Roy Peterson
Typesetting: Q Composition
Printing and Binding: Imprimerie Gagné ltée
Printed and bound in Canada

84 85 86 87 6 5 4 3 2 1

Contents

1	The man we loved to hate	7
2	A mask for all seasons	14
3	He was not always as you saw him then	33
4	When he was bad. . .	43
5	Kings 1, philosophers 0	73
6	His strength was as the strength of ten	81
7	How the West was lost	110
8	L'enfant de la patrie	116
9	Hello, cruel world	142
10	The international dream	146
11	It's time to break up, all dreams must end	176
12	The long goodbye	179

March 19, 1979

1

The man we loved to hate

IT WAS A glorious April morning in that once-upon-a-time spring of 1968 and the Pierre Elliott Trudeau who greeted me as I stepped into his as-yet-unfurnished office had just been sworn in as Canada's fifteenth prime minister. During his term in Justice, Trudeau had passed on several leaks about plans for his department. As I set up my tape recorder, I said, "Hey, I'm really glad you won the leadership. Now you'll be able to leak news to me from *all* the ministries. . . ."

"Listen," Trudeau shot back, his face suddenly hard as a death mask, "the first cabinet leak you get, I'll have the RCMP tap your phone."

Trudeau was legally correct to squash my feeble attempt to poke fun at the Privy Council oath which binds cabinet members to secrecy. But his reaction to what was obviously a tension-relieving joke was so extreme that our exchange has always stayed with me. It was a DEW-line signal of how fast and how completely power would change the man who, literally hours before, had been on the convention floor, doing the boogaloo, shrugging away his victory and kissing the girls under the shimmer of television Klieg lights.

Pierre Elliott Trudeau put us on the map. His candor, his intellectual curiosity, his nose-thumbing at the staid traditions of this country's highest political office qualified him as our first existential political hero: the man with the red rose in his buttonhole, the guy who rescued us—finally—from the age of Mackenzie King.

He saved Confederation by facing down the Front de Libération du Québec in 1970 and winning the referendum on French Canada's future a decade later. He made us all aware that politics at its best consists not of backroom deals but of sharing the passions of our age. His reign overlapped the terms of five American presidents and five

British prime ministers; he served more time in office than the combined total of nine leaders of the Conservative Party since 1919. He won four elections, kept the Liberals in power for all but nine months of the past sixteen years and accomplished precisely what he set out to do: bring home Canada's constitution and create a "new Canada" within which talented Quebeckers could take their rightful place.

Trudeau brought out the best and the worst in us, providing a catharsis from the national ennui under his nineteenth-century predecessors. He exposed our collective prejudices, regional jealousies and general stuffiness, so that when his term expired, mixed with the public jubilation was the feeling that somehow we had let *him* down, that his challenge to all of us to be a little less grey, to play it a little less safe, had gone unanswered.

This dichotomy of feeling is caught in a quote from the French essayist Jean de La Bruyère, commenting on the demise of a literary rival: "It is rumoured that Piso is dead. It is a great loss. He was a good man and deserved a longer life. He was talented, reliable, resolute and courageous, faithful and generous. Provided, of course, that he is really dead."

Though they would endure a week of blackflies before admitting it, most Canadians, at the time of Trudeau's resignation, pined a while for the delicious feeling we had when we dared elect (not as a temporary fluke, but to rule an entire generation) such a fabulous smart ass. No other country could boast of a head of government who could dance the Arab *moozmaad* in Sheik Yamani's desert tent; practice his pirouette behind the Queen's back at Buckingham Palace; yell *"Mangez la merde!"* at striking mail-truck drivers; skin-dive, high-dive and ride a unicycle; earn a brown belt in judo; date some of the world's most desirable women, marry twenty-two-year-old Margaret Sinclair, one of the local variety, and have two of his three sons, Justin and Sacha (Michel is the third son), born on the same day as Jesus Christ. Even his marriage breakup would command world attention, as Margaret "liberated" herself in the company of The Rolling Stones, the Studio 54 crowd and Manhattan's jaded jetset.

Trudeau was such an anomaly because within Official Ottawa, lucidity and frankness have always been in short supply. His deliberate vulgarisms, funny sayings, and unwillingness to fudge the accepted quota of issues left us a legacy of aphorisms:

Campaigning for the Liberal leadership on March 10, 1968, in Victoria: *An exciting Party should have both blondes and brunettes.*

To a bull at an artificial insemination centre at Milton, Ontario, on June 19, 1970: *It must be a good life.*

In an interview, when asked about his prime ministerial duties: *I'm not going to let this job louse up my private life. And I don't wear sandals around 24 Sussex Drive. I go barefoot.*

In Winnipeg on December 13, 1968, at a time of poor markets: *Well, why should I sell the Canadian farmers' wheat?*

When asked in April 1970 about Canada's policy on Biafra: *Where's Biafra?*

That last quotation—used more frequently than any other to demonstrate Trudeau's arrogance, because Biafrans were starving—illustrates how even the most offhand of his comments had a deeper meaning. Unlike 99.9 percent of Canadians, Trudeau knew precisely where Biafra was, having visited that region of Nigeria during a world tour in the 1950s. But his government's policy was to recognize Nigeria, not its breakaway province. Ever-conscious of a Quebec that was pushing for separate international status, Trudeau was trying to underline his view that, legally, Biafra didn't exist, and that questions about it were comparable to asking, "Where is Laurentia?"—the name French-Canadian nationalists sometimes gave to their dream of an independent state.

But even more than by his words, Trudeau was defined by his gestures—the man's body language is worthy of a doctoral thesis in linguistics. He was always the dancing man sliding down banisters, dodging (or slugging) picketers, hopping on or off platforms (some say *fences*). And then there was the chilly topography of his face, his intelligent, devilish countenance, unlined by what Balzac called "private defeats," offset by eyes the depth and color of the sea. As Global-TV's Doug Small phrased it, Trudeau's is "an aboriginal face." Marshall McLuhan had said "tribal."

In a television age when most stars feel lucky if they last the season, Trudeau's hold on the Canadian imagination was only magnified by time. He became a kind of resident Canadian wizard, a cool man in a hot world doing his grainy thing.

Looking back on this remarkable prime minister and his times, it seems clear that we burdened him with expectations no mortal could meet. There *had* to be a gap between his intentions and deeds, between his promise and his performance. But that didn't explain why he became such a lightning rod for our complaints, the most despised prime minister in our history. I remember watching with fascination a burly trucker at a motel near Red Deer who had lost his forty-five cents in a Coke vending machine. He stood back and kicked the thing. Nothing happened. He shook it nearly off the hinges. No luck. Then he took a deep breath, glared at the offending contraption and cursed, "God *damn* Trudeau anyway!"—and walked away.

No realist thought that Pierre Trudeau would in fact become a philosopher-king. Politics in Canada has always been the art of making the necessary possible, and all of our successful prime ministers quickly became adept at pragmatic improvisation. What we did have the right to expect in Trudeau was a man with a creative urge to heal, a leader who would not only tolerate but encourage discussion and dissent.

Trudeau's trouble was that he saw himself as a Charles de Gaulle of the Rideau and, like the French general, he believed that a man's grandeur grows in direct proportion to his aloofness. Trudeau in office remained an emotional cripple—a supremely detached Jesuit with a splinter of ice in his heart. If it was true that John Diefenbaker too often "thought with his heart," it was equally true that Pierre Trudeau too frequently "felt with his mind," leaving the impression that he didn't give a damn.

Throughout the Trudeau Years, Canadian voters waited in vain for that magic moment when Pierre would wake to realize that mind was not enough to revive his divided and economically downcast country. But compassion remained a quality that did not cast much of a shadow on his interior landscape. Trudeau in office was a Zen adept who could detach himself from whatever was happening around him, judging or not judging as he wished.

Despite his shimmering intellect and a resoluteness of purpose unmatched by any Canadian political leader, Trudeau operated out of a very deep fallacy: he tended to stifle dissent. Tolerating dissent is an essential means by which a society comes to terms with change, but the prime minister and his inner circle seemed to believe that they could impose logic on events, that they could govern the country through legalism and reshape events to fit those legalisms. However, events themselves are never logical; history is born out of harsh realities and even harder emotions which cannot be cut to fit a leader's wishes or good intentions.

Trudeau could never grasp the fundamental animating spirit of Canadian democracy: that political parties in this country are not ideological armies but temporary coalitions of disparate men and women, in it not for glory but for fun. To him, politics had to provide intellectual stimulation and/or satisfaction. Period. The idea that bored housewives from the Soo became Liberals because party functions transmogrified them into vaguely officious charmers, or that unkempt carousers from St. Boniface belonged to the party because they saw themselves as heavy-duty primetime guys at policy conferences—the very notion that anyone would go into politics except as an act of duty to the state baffled and escaped the leader's ken. As a result, during the first part of his run Trudeau almost invariably picked the wrong political advisors—earnest inferior P.E.T. clones who transmitted to him no sense of country. They were men and women with voices and intuitions that echoed his own.

In their determination to intellectualize Canadian politics, most of Trudeau's Bright Young Courtiers were caught up in a cocoon of their own making, responding to in-group logic instead of to real events. They became Trudeau's royal court and, like all sycophants mistook the chatter of the palace for the voice of the people. They saw public service as the reduction of issues to manageable proportions and unconsciously modelled themselves on McGeorge Bundy, the Kennedy White House advisor who once explained that "man's real motivating force is the simple, natural, almost unexamined human desire to do something really well." But he never said what.

During those early years, the three men closest to Trudeau were Marc Lalonde, the PM's principal secretary, Jim Davey, a Cambridge physics grad who became program secretary and introduced flow charts and systems analysis into the PMO, and Ivan Head, a Harvard man and former law professor who wrote speeches for Trudeau that read like drafts of monographs for *Foreign Affairs* instead of folksy patter for Legion halls. (Their idea of being good partisans was to cut off anyone who questioned their judgement or showed the slightest sign of dissent. At the start of the 1968 election, Jim Davey sent a memo to John Nichol, then in charge of the campaign, recommending that Trudeau limit his appearances to constituencies represented by MPs or delegates who had supported his run for the leadership. Lalonde intercepted the memorandum and scissored out that particular passage, so it never reached Liberal headquarters.)

After the shock of winning only a minority mandate in 1972, the coterie of Trudeau advisors did not, as might have been expected, lose their influence. On the contrary. The inner circle among his trusted advisors became even smaller, because Trudeau stopped trying to reach out to any outsiders. "There was a strong passive quality in the man," recalled a senior bureaucrat once very close to Trudeau. "People would drift away from him and he would never once ask them to stay. He would see an old friend at a party and say, 'You know, we really must get together some time,' but he wouldn't follow it up."

The Trudeau court lived and worked in an environment as cloistered as a high-walled Gobi Desert treasure city before Marco Polo came by. What they forgot was that in a democracy, the minority's dissent is just as important as the majority's assent; that thoughts and feelings, however untidy, must be gathered from many sources and can never be irrelevant to the exercise of power. Before he became prime minister, Trudeau had travelled the country on the slogan that he was looking for "new guys with new ideas." Once in power, he behaved as though he wanted "new guys with the same ideas"—the same as his own.

As the Trudeau Years rolled on and the voices of disorder began bellowing their demands even louder, his advisors felt threatened and began to play everything safe, placing the avoidance of disaster ahead of legislative adventures; their operational code became "Always the Lesser Evil." They saw themselves as defenders of social structures within which citizens would keep their proper place.

This retreat to a redefined status quo was disrupted by the ascendancy of Keith Davey, who virtually took over the management of Trudeau's political life. He was the first member of the prime minister's entourage who could qualify as an agitator—willing to joke with Trudeau and remind him that he was human and fallible.

Until then, it had been a court without a jester.

Keith Davey filled the role of court jester not because he was in any sense a clown but, like his wise predecessors in Shakespeare's plays, he delivered uncomfortable truths in candy wrappings. He understood that any effective prime minister needs a "kitchen" cabinet of cronies even more than a brains trust, and that a good politician must "think with his liver."

Davey's critics in the party claimed his idea of the Canada that mattered was everything he could see from Toronto's CN Tower, but there were few others within the Trudeau circle who had the capacity to get angry when a situation was not merely illogical but unjust. This was hardly surprising, since most of the men and women who surrounded and cosseted Pierre Trudeau while he was in power seldom came closer to personal discomfort than having to suffer through bad service at one of Ottawa's many declining restaurants.

For his own part, Trudeau demonstrated over and over again that he regarded the job of prime minister as quite separate from his inner self. It was almost as though he got up each morning and cast himself in his role, putting on the various masks appropriate to the occasion. Such theatrics seemed to drain him of an appropriate repertoire of emotions. It was as if he had a mail-order soul. (When there were close to a million Canadians out of work, Trudeau rose in the House of Commons (April 16, 1970) and casually mused about unemployment as "a very regrettable side effect of inflation.")

Caught between militant demands and moderate possibilities, Trudeau retreated into petulance. His attitude was reminiscent of nothing so much as a description of Francis Bacon by Lytton Strachey, who wrote that "Bacon's intelligence was external. He could understand almost everything except his own heart."

I recall the time I was discussing the prime minister with Gordon Fairweather (later named the first chairman of Canada's Human Rights Commission but then an Opposition MP from New Brunswick), who commanded enormous respect and affection in Official Ottawa. When the Trudeaus had given birth to one of their December 25 babies, Fairweather was delighted. In a burst of bonhomie, he went down to his local post office on Boxing Day to send a congratulatory wire. In the post office the telegrapher, a true-blue Tory, said she didn't want to transmit the message. She tried to get Fairweather to give up on it. He wouldn't, and found the whole episode quite funny, a vignette of his riding's style. When the House session opened in January, he went up to Trudeau at the usual Speaker's cocktail party and tried to tell him what had happened, thinking Trudeau might find it amusing. Trudeau simply stared back at him, bored, and said—as though he thought Fairweather was fishing for a thank-you for the telegram—"Oh, I never saw it. There were so many hundreds of them we decided not to be bothered."

Fairweather later commented that he felt not so much hurt as punctured—as though he had been punched in the chest, hard.

And yet there were moments when Trudeau *did* show his feelings, such as during his first resignation on November 21, 1979. When he walked into the Liberal caucus room that day, only Marc Lalonde knew what was about to happen. Monique Bégin, sensing something was up, whispered to a colleague: "*Il y a le malheur à la porte.*" ("Misfortune is at the door.") Trudeau pulled several sheets of paper out of his pocket and in a flat voice started to read: "I am announcing today that after spending nearly twelve years as leader of the Liberal Party, I am stepping down from the leadership . . ." Then he broke into tears, weeping too hard to finish.

2

A mask for all seasons

When put on the defensive, he leaped to the offensive—
in every sense of the word.

August 9, 1982

April 9, 1975

April Showers

July 18, 1977

NATIONAL UNITY
CANADIAN $
RCMP BREAK-INS
INFLATION
UNEMPLOYMENT

October 11, 1977

November 2, 1977

Above the law

December 19, 1977

February 24, 1978

February 25, 1978

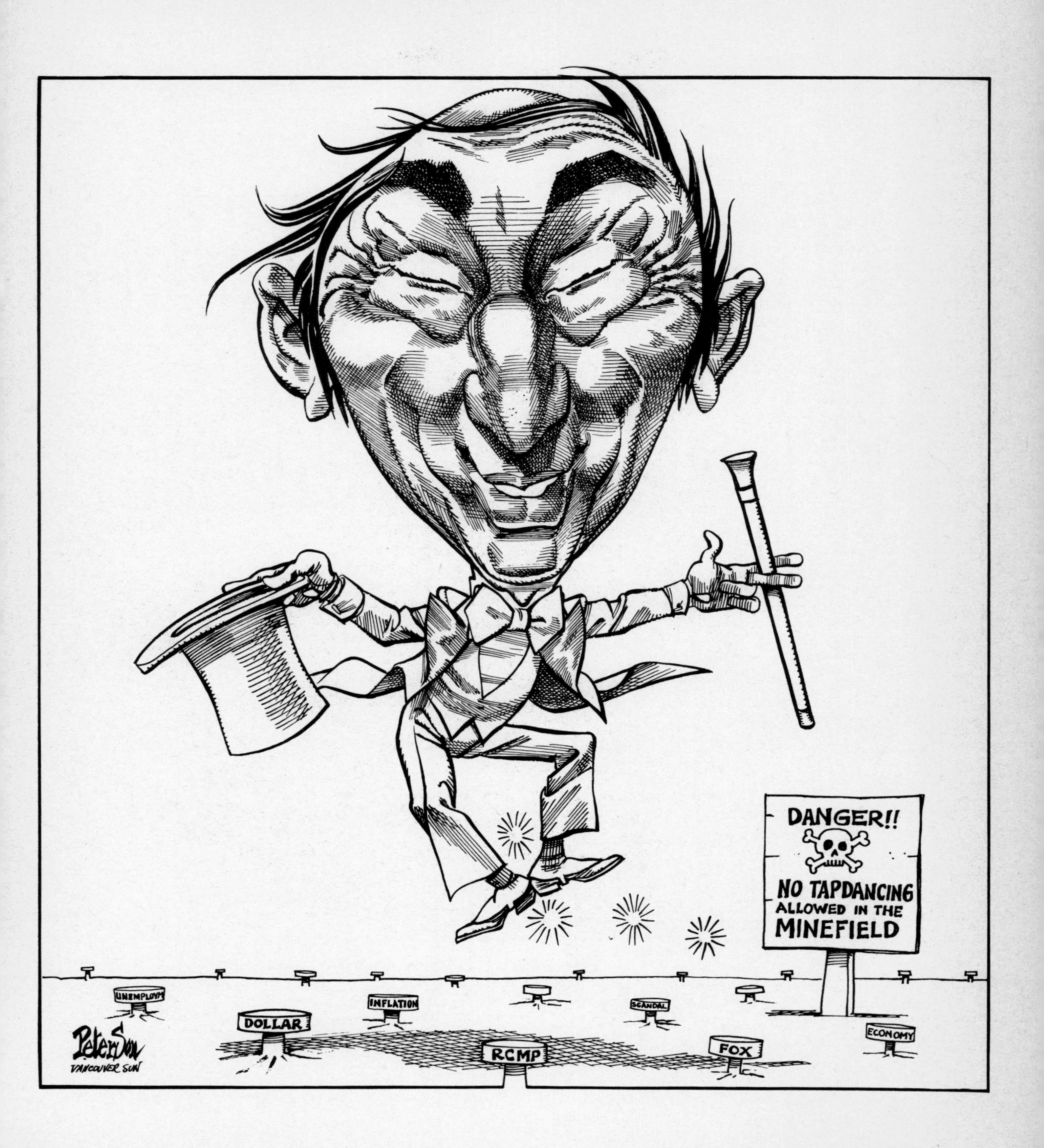

June 2, 1978

August 21, 1978

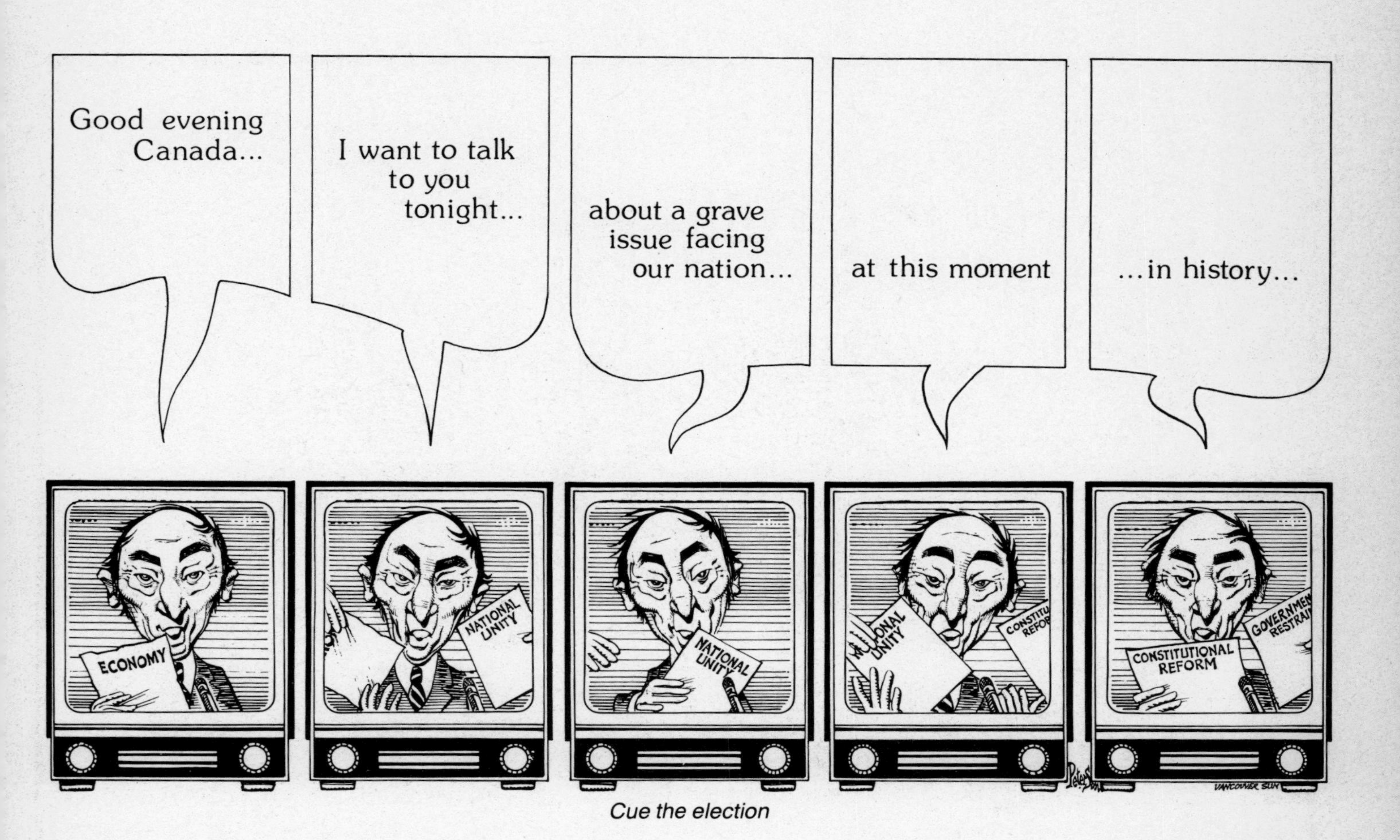

Cue the election

December 10, 1980

January 13, 1982

July 23, 1982

OVER A MILLION UNEMPLOYED, $7 BILLION FOR JOBLESS BENEFITS, A STRANGLED ECONOMY, A FLOPPING DOLLAR, A $20 BILLION DEFICIT, WHAT DO YOU INTEND TO DO ABOUT IT ?
YOU HAVE ALL THE ANSWERS DON'T YOU, PIERRE ?
JOE, WHAT DO YOU SAY WE TAKE A COMMONS BREAK AND GO ON VACATION ?
PETERSON
VANCOUVER SUN

August 11, 1982

"... as this unretouched photo shows ... the prime minister was merely pointing out the government's relocation scheme for those Canadians seeking employment in other parts of the country ..."

December 15, 1982

"The trick of course, Ebenezer, is to stimulate the economy without actually using money . . ."

June 29, 1983

". . . and although massive unemployment is still rampant, I'd like to praise all those Canadians within the sound of my voice for their cooperation in our constant battle against inflation . . ."

August 19, 1983

". . . well Sacha, you just tell Mr. Zorba that we're NOT in exile but on an official state visit paid for by the Canadian taxpayer!"

February 17, 1984

August 30, 1982

3

He was not always as you saw him then

PIERRE ELLIOTT TRUDEAU appeared out of nowhere like a desert prince who knows the magic of the shifting sands. In fact, he was the product of a crammed, precisely plotted education that included stints at Harvard, the Sorbonne, the London School of Economics and the University of Montreal—immersion that didn't end until he entered active politics at the age of forty-six.

His father Charles-Emile was a farmer's son who earned a law degree and established a chain of gasoline stations on Montreal Island, which he later sold to Imperial Oil in 1932 for $1.4 million. The funds were re-invested so wisely that Pierre (born on October 18, 1919), his sister Suzette and brother Charles each became multimillionaires. If his father taught him order and discipline, his mother, the former Grace Elliott, imbued him with a longing for freedom and the appreciation of fantasy. At Collège Jean-de-Brébeuf, an elite centre for the Jesuit teaching order in Montreal, he absorbed the mysteries of the Catholic will. It was there, too, that he began to excel at individual sports—high-diving, judo, skiing, gymnastics and canoeing. Then followed years of study at the University of Montreal (he was called to the Quebec Bar in 1943); at Harvard ("I realized we were being taught law as a trade in Quebec, not as a discipline. The majors in political science at Harvard had read more about Roman Law and Montesquieu than I as a lawyer."); at the Ecole des Sciences Politiques at the Sorbonne; and with the influential Harold Laski at the London School of Economics. The affiliations outside of Canada were later held against him, with right-wing journalists and fascist pamphleteers ascribing pinko influences to Harvard ("a spawning ground of leftist intellectuals") and Laski (labelled "a Marxist"). No one took the trouble to remark on the fact that former Conservative leader Robert Stanfield and half the Canadian business Establishment had also put in time at Harvard, or that Laski, while a member in good standing of the Fabian Society and chairman of the British Labour Party, was not a Communist.

In the two years that followed his "formal" education, Trudeau travelled the world in solitary quest to taste new cultures and languages. The exact chronology of that time is unclear. For example, in no recitation of his tours is Italy mentioned, yet I vividly recall attending an election rally with Trudeau in a Toronto riding during which he was asked a question in Italian. Without skipping a beat he replied in what sounded like perfect Italian, then switched back to English; as far as I know, he never spoke Italian publicly again.

His known ports of call included Belgrade, Vienna, Budapest, Istanbul, Warsaw, much of the Middle East, India and Pakistan. He was expelled from Yugoslavia as an Israeli spy and penetrated Palestine aboard a truck of renegade Arabs, just before Partition in 1948.

Trudeau returned to Canada in 1949 and, finding that Cardinal Léger had vetoed his application to teach political theory at the church-controlled University of Montreal, joined the Privy Council office in Ottawa, under Louis St. Laurent. The next three years made a deep impression on the young cosmopolitan: even though the prime minister of the day was from Quebec City, most French Canadians at that time occupied token positions within the federal bureaucracy and French was used mainly by elevator operators and the maitre d' at Madame Burger's Restaurant in Hull.

During the 1950s, Trudeau founded the intellectual review *Cité Libre*, and resumed his globe-trotting. Once again, his Montreal publishing activities and travels would be retroactively condemned by critics who didn't bother checking their facts. A few examples illustrate the discrepancies.

• *The Charge*: that as editor of *Cité Libre* he featured works of Professor Raymond Boyer (convicted of Soviet espionage in the Gouzenko case); Stanley B. Ryerson, the leading theoretician of the Canadian Communist Party; and Pierre Gélinas, the Quebec director of the Communist Party's agitation and propaganda section.

• *The Facts*: Raymond Boyer did contribute two articles to *Cité Libre*—in December 1952 and May 1955, one dealing with a study of the death penalty in New France and another with a history of torture through the ages; as well, he wrote some literary reviews. Ryerson did not contribute to the magazine. The Gélinas article was published in 1952 as part of a review of a recent provincial election campaign in which he described Communist Party involvement.

• *The Charge*: that Trudeau was picked up in 1961 by the U.S. Coast Guard off Key West, Florida, trying to run guns to Castro's Cuba in a small boat.

• *The Facts*: Trudeau and two friends—Alphonse Gagnon and Valmore Francoeur—did join in an attempt to row a small boat across the Straits of Florida to Cuba. Their objective was to test the boat, invented by Gagnon, which used footpedals instead of oars. They were stopped by the U.S. Coast Guard because they had passed the off-shore limits, and because a storm was brewing and the Americans were concerned about their safety. After some discussion, the Coast Guard let them continue in the company of a shrimp boat. (The storm eventually forced them to turn back.)

• *The Charge*: that in 1952 Trudeau led a delegation of Communists to the International Economic Conference in Moscow.

• *The Facts*: Trudeau did attend the Conference (but not as the leader of any delegation) as did many respected economists of several Western countries. He caused a minor riot in Moscow's Red Square when he started to heave snowballs at the then-hallowed statue of Joseph Stalin. He was let off with a warning when he explained to some puzzled policemen that whenever he went to Ottawa he threw snowballs at the statue of Sir Wilfrid Laurier.

• *The Charge*: that in 1960 Trudeau led a Communist delegation to Peking for a Red victory celebration.

• *The Facts*: Trudeau's China trip was not at the head of any delegation but in the company of Jacques Hébert, the Montreal publisher. The story of their journey was published in a benign travel book, *Deux Innocents en Chine Rouge*.

• *The Charge*: that in 1952 Trudeau was barred entry into the United States as an inadmissible person.

• *The Facts*: Under a U. S. immigration regulation, all individuals who had travelled behind the Iron Curtain later than 1946 were barred entry. But once Trudeau explained the nature of his trip to the American consul in Montreal, the ban was lifted.

During the mid-1950s, Trudeau's *Cité Libre* became an important agent in rallying intellectual dissent against the increasingly oppressive regime of Maurice Duplessis. He also founded a pseudo-political movement named *Le Rassemblement* (which was dedicated to uniting opposition to the Union Nationale) and supported the Liberals in the 1960 election which brought a reform-minded Jean Lesage into power. In a prophetic essay written at the time, Trudeau commented: "If, in the last analysis, we continually identify Catholicism with conservatism, and patriotism with immobility, we will lose by default that which is at play between all cultures . . . An entire generation is hesitating at the brink of commitment."

The Trudeau of this period developed a reputation for skipping from cause to cause, idea to idea. His fellow Quebec "wise man," Jean Marchand, then the province's most militant union leader, once testified that, "Pierre . . . took a long time to get involved in things. In any social or political adventure he had to overcome a considerable reluctance. As soon as he felt he was menaced with involvement, he left for the south of France." But despite his long absences, Trudeau did start to build up a following among young teachers and lawyers in the province and managed to publish several books and some fifty articles, including an epochal appeal for realism in Canadian politics, published simultaneously in *Cité Libre* and *The Canadian Forum*. (The document was translated by a close friend of Trudeau's named Michael Pitfield, then working for the Governor General in Ottawa.)

I remember calling on Trudeau at the time. He was working in a bare cubicle at the University of Montreal's Institute for Public Law, wearing outrageously ill-matched clothes. He told me that separatism in Quebec would never triumph because it could not transform itself into a broadly based popular movement. Instead, it had become what Trudeau called "a bourgeois revolution—the uprising of people who were afraid they wouldn't have enough important jobs in the society of tomorrow. They thought that only an independent Quebec would solve their problem, because they would be its new elite and wouldn't have to share power and jobs with outsiders."

When Trudeau, Gérard Pelletier and Jean Marchand became candidates in the 1965 election, it was considered a great coup for Prime Minister Lester Pearson. At a time when support of the federal interest was an unpopular posture in their own milieu, these gallant, middle-aged ex-revolutionaries took a risky stand, clearly identifying themselves as Quebeckers who believed in the Canadian future. This was no easy decision for a trio whose professional lives had been devoted to fostering the social upheaval that became Quebec's "quiet revolution." By joining Ottawa and the federal Liberals, they were rejecting the notion that the government of Quebec should be the solitary custodian of French-Canadian rights.

Despite his public championing of Quebec's contemporary aspirations, Pearson had been nearly as guilty as his predecessors in declining to admit a single French Canadian into the inner circle of political power. While he had more Quebec ministers in his administration than any previous Canadian government, not a single one of the then "Big Six" ministries (Finance, Trade and Commerce, External Affairs, Defence, Health and Welfare, Transport) had been given to a French Canadian. (The only senior portfolio held by a Quebec minister was Justice, and it had more prestige than power.) There was only one French Canadian on the prime minister's staff above stenographic rank (his secretary, Jules Pelletier), and the ingrained Ottawa attitude of giving only the trappings of power to French Canadians pervaded the civil service as well. Of the three dozen or so top-level bureaucrats who formed "the Ottawa Establishment," only one deputy minister—Marcel Cadieux, Under-Secretary of State for External Affairs—was a French Canadian. In the eleven most important departments, only six of the 163 civil servants who received $14,000 a year or more were from French Canada.

The entry into active federal politics of Marchand, Pelletier and Trudeau transformed the attitudes that produced such an obvious imbalance. In the past, Quebec lieutenants such as Lionel Chevrier, Maurice Lamontagne and Guy Favreau had diverted French Canada's true aspirations into the service of the province's vested economic interests and the dispensation of political patronage. The trio of Montreal newcomers, together with their like-minded colleagues, Maurice Sauvé and Jean-Luc Pépin, was determined to claim the substance and not just the illusion of federal power. Trudeau was promoted within months of arriving in Ottawa. On January 9, 1966, he was named parliamentary assistant to the prime minister; he served on several important committees, represented Canada at the 21st Session of the United Nations General Assembly in New York, and headed a task force on the possibility of changing Canada's constitution. He grew personally close to the prime minister and was thus excused from the usual apprenticeship in the anterooms of power reserved for most fledgling MPs.

Pearson recognized in Trudeau a man very different from the many florid French Canadians who had preceded him. Despite Trudeau's deliberate eccentricities of dress, he possessed the qualities Pearson admired. He was the product of a rich and cultivated home, he had been educated abroad, had travelled widely, was an avowed intellectual, a sometime reformer and a convinced internationalist.

On April 4, 1967, Trudeau was appointed Minister of Justice and Attorney General of Canada, and he set about trying to reform a badly outdated justice system. During an interview I had with him at the time, he went directly to the core of his political philosophies: "This should be regarded more and more as a department planning for the society of tomorrow, not merely acting as the government's legal advisor. It should combine the function of drafting new legislation with the disciplines of sociology and economics, so that it can provide a framework for our evolving way of life . . . we have to move the framework of society slightly ahead of the times . . ."

Eight months later, he presented a reform package to the Commons and, while defending his ideas on television, mumbled the magic phrase: "I want to separate sin from crime. You may have to ask forgiveness for your sins from God, but not from the Minister of Justice. There's no place for the state in the bedrooms of the nation."

This was hardly a startling proposition, but it made a disproportionate impact on an electorate numbed by generations of politicians blowing through their moustaches about the gross national product and federal-provincial relations. It was the first intimation that Trudeau might be able to excite public opinion.

With Pearson on the verge of resignation, a lively debate was starting within the Quebec wing of the Liberal Party about the advisability of their entry into the leadership race. The party had alternated French and English prime ministers since Confederation, but the commonly held view of the moment was that the concessions demanded by Quebec would be more acceptable to the rest of Canada if they were put forward by an English-speaking leader. At the same time, it was said that if a French Canadian did try for the succession and lost (or won the leadership but was defeated in the election that followed), it would be interpreted as a serious insult to French Canada. Most Ottawa Liberals argued that the Quebec ministers, instead of putting up a candidate of their own, should form a bloc, pick an English-speaking minister and bargain off their support in return for some specific policy commitments and the promise of at least two senior economic portfolios in the new leader's cabinet.

This was not the view held by the small but resolute band of Quebec Liberals who tried to get Jean Marchand to run, but when he decided that neither his command of English nor his health were really up to it, Trudeau became the centre of their attention.

If Pierre Trudeau's subsequent conquest of the Liberal Party appears in retrospect to have been predestined, with the other contenders for the leadership serving as mere flag-bearers, in the bleak chill of December 1967, just after Lester Pearson's resignation, Trudeau's victory seemed far from inevitable. In fact, it was scarcely credible. To most Liberals, Trudeau was an untested outsider, a disturbing presence not easily encompassed by the collective party mind.

Rideau Club denizens were fond of telling each other the story about the time he turned up on a Saturday morning at the Privy Council Office dressed in desert boots and a boiler suit. The commissionaire on duty, convinced he was a plumber who had his worksheets jumbled, turned him away at the door. When his name was mentioned casually in the early speculative talk about candidates, it was dismissed as a joke. ("How could anybody who combs his hair like that be a Canadian prime minister?")

In this uncertain preliminary stage, the contest for the succession was little more than sentiment in search of a leader. Many Liberals felt they wanted a dramatic change from the Pearson brand of politics, a candidate who could reestablish public trust in the party and the party's confidence in itself. But it was difficult to identify this urge with any of the obvious contenders so eagerly offering themselves for the job. Most of them—Paul Hellyer, Mitchell Sharp, Paul Martin, Robert Winters, Allan MacEachen, Joe Greene—seemed to represent the old instead of the new politics. And of the others, John Turner was too untried, and Eric Kierans' power base owed more to decency than delegate strength.

As well, in the disturbing decade since Pearson's anointment, changes in the Canadian social structure had splintered the Liberal Party hierarchy. The machine politicians, smoky-room lawyers, bagman senators and cabinet ministers with a talent for back-concession politicking, who had once been able to "deliver" whole provinces, could no longer do so. Party authority at the constituency level had been disseminated among large groups of younger political activists who were not so readily predictable or so easily controllable.

In English Canada, MPs, historians, communicators and progressive thinkers of every stripe were coalescing behind a Trudeau candidacy. Toronto artist Mashel Teitelbaum started circulating a petition which eventually comprised six hundred big-name signatures. In a courting mood, but not committing himself, Trudeau left for a holiday in the South Pacific. "Before I make my decision," he told a friend, "I've got to find out whether it's really possible to *do* anything once I get in the prime minister's office."

Following Trudeau's triumphant tour of the country selling a new constitutional reform package, and after his star performance at a federal-provincial conference (where he bested Quebec Premier Daniel Johnson), his candidacy became an accepted fact. On February 14, 1968, he called a press conference to announce it, leaving little doubt that he would be a very different candidate from those who'd gone before. After accusing the media of "creating" his candidacy as a joke on the Liberal Party, he concluded: ". . . when I saw the response from political people, from members of the party and responsible members of Parliament, this is when I began to wonder if this whole thing was not a bit more serious than you and I had intended. . . . It looks a bit like when I tried to enter the party. I didn't think the Liberal Party would take [me]—and suddenly, they did. So I was stuck with it. Well, now you're stuck with me."

Almost immediately, the race became Trudeau against all the others. His popularity soared; even his fellow contenders did not dare attack him, though Paul Martin was privately comparing his candidacy to George Bernard Shaw's running for the Conservative leadership in Britain—an intimation that the Justice Minister was both a dilettante and a Fabian socialist.

Riding a chartered jet and wearing a leather coat, Trudeau travelled twenty thousand miles, making thirty stops, during his leadership campaign. Every appearance brought standing ovations. He seemed able, without strain, to establish personal contact with his audiences, operating on a private wavelength the other candidates couldn't jam.

The difference between the Canada that created Lester Pearson and the Canada that overwhelmed him was nowhere more visible than in the contrast between the way he was chosen leader in 1958 and how Pierre Elliott Trudeau gained power in 1968. In that decade, the nation had undergone a revolution and the world that had bestowed the leadership on Lester Pearson like a garland had vanished.

In January 1958, Pearson had run his leadership campaign without leaving Ottawa. He had taken rooms at the Château Laurier Hotel, met key delegates and exchanged confidences without ever actually giving the impression that he was campaigning. Paul Martin, his only serious rival, was criticized at the time for boldly turning up at the Ottawa railway station to shake the hands of arriving dignitaries.

The convention that year was held in the Ottawa Coliseum, still fragrant from a recent livestock show and decorated for the political occasion with bunting and large studio portrait blow-ups of Laurier, St. Laurent and King. It was a low-key spectacle, where senators still counted and the only touch of color was provided by a few University of Toronto students in sober business suits and pearly girls in cashmere sweaters shouting "Hurrah for Mike!" Television coverage was subdued and limited mainly to Pearson's acceptance speech delivered after his easy first-ballot win.

By 1968 television had taken over the convention. Because TV screens can accommodate only one image at a time and tend to give all events equal significance, Trudeau stood to gain the most from the coverage. From the moment he entered the race, the managers of the electronic media made an instinctive decision that he would be the winner, and their message was not lost on the delegates. Throughout the convention eight camera crews clustered about the Justice Minister, ignoring most of the other candidates much of the time—giving Trudeau the advantage of built-in excitement, and bathing him in a constant halo of artificial light. His emotional impact had been demonstrated most forcefully when he arrived for the convention by train: girls had thrown wedding rice, waved Valentines and squeaked in delight, gasping for the sight of him. "Something happens to people's faces when they see Trudeau," Ron Haggart wrote in the *Toronto Star*. "You can manufacture noise and screaming kids, but you cannot manufacture that excitement in the eyes . . . It's not madness, not in these excited matrons and lawyers. It is belief."

Recruiting delegates, Trudeau was completely at ease with himself and with his audiences. He did again what he had done for so many years as a university lecturer—combined theoretical musings with leaps of intuition, classical references with colloquial quips. To the familiar posture of seasoned academic were added the touches of professional performer. This involved run-on jokes and calculated mannerisms—putting his hand in his watchpocket, sipping water whenever he wanted a moment to think, raising his eyebrows to indicate that he and the questioner didn't need to add to the complexities of human existence by creating new ones. And—always—the exaggerated shrugs.

These and other tricks of stagecraft, beautifully exploited, were combined with repartee:

Trudeau: "I hope to be a prime minister who doesn't resemble in every way the Pierre Elliott Trudeau of up to now."

Question: "And how will you change?"

Trudeau: "Well, I'll have more regular hours."

Trudeau then did not so much have the knack of capturing people's hearts or minds—he was always too standoffish for that—but of connecting subliminally with their nervous systems. Standing beside a Liberal housewife at a party function in the Château Laurier in Ottawa during that first campaign, I noticed that just before Trudeau was due to be ushered through the door she stiffened, turned to her huge block of a side-burned husband and wailed, "What if I faint when he comes in?" The husband smoothed down his Brylcremed locks and rolled his eyes heavenward in a look of total disgust. When Trudeau loped by and happened to shake the man's hand, his eyes glazed over and he quietly started to cry. It was as though Trudeau was performing what Norman Mailer described as "the indispensable psychic act of a leader, who takes national anxieties so long buried and releases them to the surface where they belong." This was the mystery that made him the source of such fascination, the trick that the professionals running the other campaigns could not duplicate.

In Trudeau's offhand statements ("What we need are new guys and new ideas"), in his very presence, the delegates thought they recognized that Canada under his leadership would no longer be a tired matron clinging to the past. He seemed to hold out the promise that the process of discovering Canada had not come to an end, that Expo 67 wasn't just a momentary phenomenon, that this was still a young nation with vast, unexploited possibilities. He personified the hoped-for sophistication of the perfectly bicultural Canada of tomorrow. Not only was he comfortably fluent in both English and French, but his manner combined Gallic touches with something of the phlegm of the British upper classes—the unflappability that once built an empire.

All through that incredible circus, Trudeau maintained his inner repose, refusing to dissolve his personality or lend himself to the gravitational pull of the convention. And the more he held back, the more the crowd wanted a piece of him.

The climax came with his appearance on the convention floor. As if pulled by a single string, Trudeau signs were silently lifted in every part of the crowded arena. The delegates, instead of applauding, let out a collective "AAAHH," a salute to a daring trapeze artist doing his star turn. Although the demonstration had been carefully planned, it looked spontaneous, as though the Liberal Party had reached its pro-Trudeau consensus at that exact moment. Trudeau waited in the stands for precisely five minutes, then moved toward the platform. He talked about a Just Society, about strife in the world, about Canada's internal divisions, about each man's share of the eternal burden. "As Liberals," he said, "we rely on that most unlikely bulwark against chaos—you and me, the individual citizen, the young and the old, the famous and the unknown, the Arctic nomad and the suburbanite." He confirmed his belief in the triumph of reason over passion in politics. This was the sober, not the witty, Pierre, softly blowing his own horn. At the end of his speech he stood there, smiling, with his rounded Edwardian collar and a daffodil in his buttonhole, the candidate assured of victory.

The election that followed was a combination of coronation and Beatles tour. Teeny-boppers with manes of streaming hair gripped their machine-autographed photos of Pierre-baby to their chests and shrieked whenever he deigned to kiss one of their swarming number. Bemused toddlers borne on their parents' shoulders were admonished to "remember him," as excitement surged across the country. Press cameras whirred like hungry electronic crickets every time Trudeau stepped from his prime ministerial jet, Caesar haircut intact, to make his triumphant way from one shopping centre plaza to the next.

I recall in particular one landing in Dartmouth, Nova Scotia. We in his media entourage trudged down the plane's steps into a cold, drizzly night. That was wall-to-wall Tory country, but along the route from the airport, as if on a prearranged signal, people came out on their porches to wave at the procession. Many had backed their cars into their driveways so that they could flash their headlights in silent salute to "the great man." In Victoria, where the monarchy was still an important issue, local Liberals questioned Trudeau closely on a topic he had previously dismissed as irrelevant. He won the crowd over with a shrug and the comment: "I was in Saskatoon last night and crowned a lovely queen, so I feel warm toward the monarchy."

There was a certain shock value in his appearance. Voters came prepared to be fascinated and scandalized by a wild man in sandals spouting socialist slogans. Instead they found an immaculate, demure professor delivering proposals that sounded exciting but would not have been out of place in any Canadian Manufacturers' Association brief. Unable to classify him as a man of either the political right or the political left, most of Trudeau's listeners seemed happy to regard him simply as a man of the future.

Awarded a conclusive majority (155 of 264 seats), Trudeau set out to govern a country which had, in effect, given him a blank cheque.

4

When he was bad . . .

He may not be around to kick any more, but he got kicked pretty hard when he was.

January 17, 1976

November 20, 1972

"Speaking of seasonal adjustments — what is your party standing this week?"

July 15, 1974

"What, me defect, when you've just signed a long-run contract?"

September 30, 1974

March 31, 1975

The Sugaring-off Ceremony

April 15, 1975

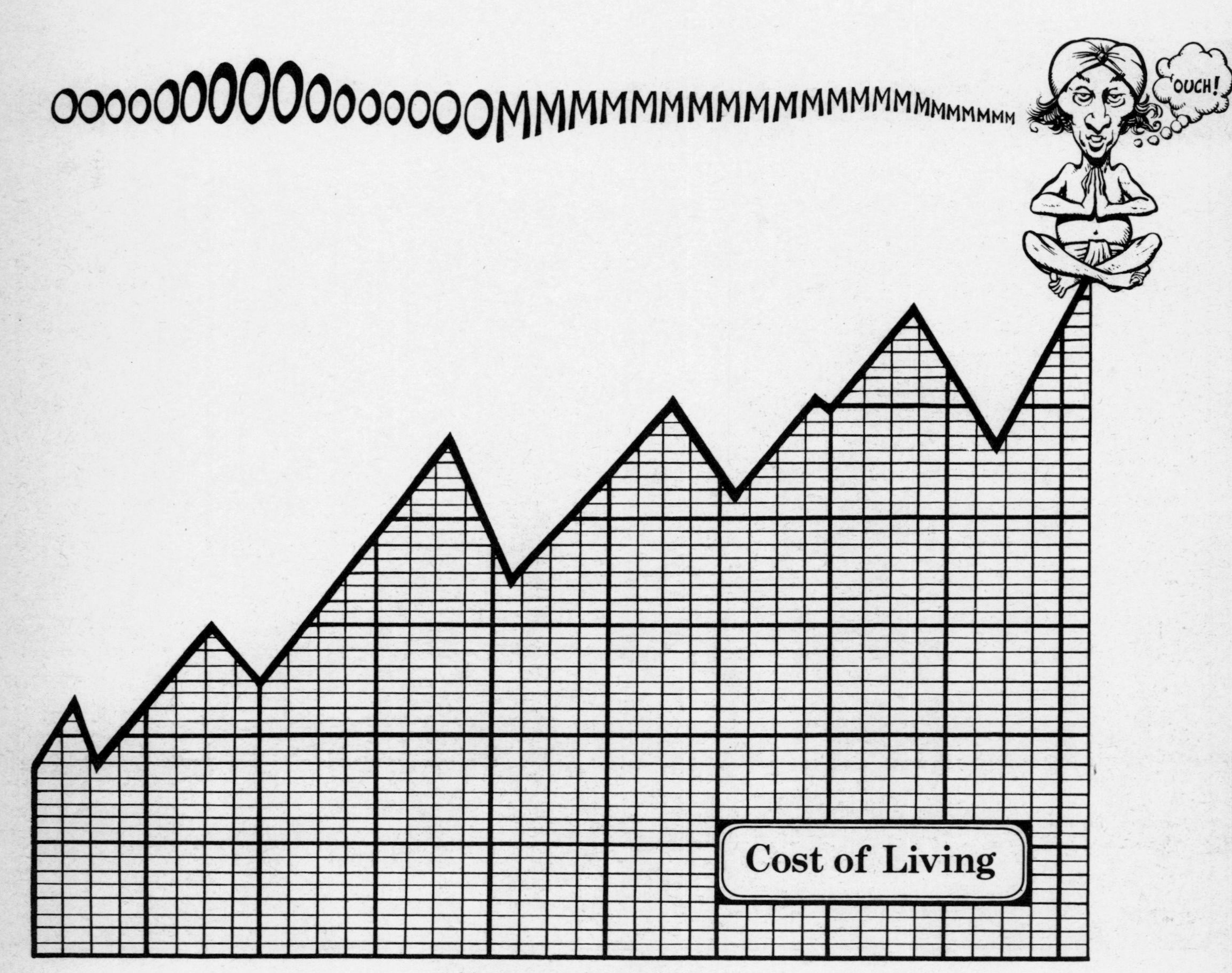

Matter over mind

April 16, 1975

His master's vice

April 17, 1975

"Don't move! We've got a 33½ per cent pay hike for me and Turner's working on a May budget for you! We can battle them off together!"

" The good news is that your universe is unfolding as it should. The bad news is that fewer people believe in the old unfolding universe schtik. "

November 17, 1975

...without a paddle

September 13, 1976

The Bionic Man

KING CANUTE
PRICES
& WAGES
MOSES AND THE RED SEA
Peterson

March 17, 1977

October 17, 1977

October 20, 1977

Tag Team

May 13, 1978

August 26, 1978

September 5, 1978

"Oh yes, ruling by divine right has worked out pretty well so far, but frankly, I could use some divine intervention in the next few months . . . ."

September 25, 1978

"Enough of this provincial election analysis. What news of the public mood, Coutts?"

August 6, 1981

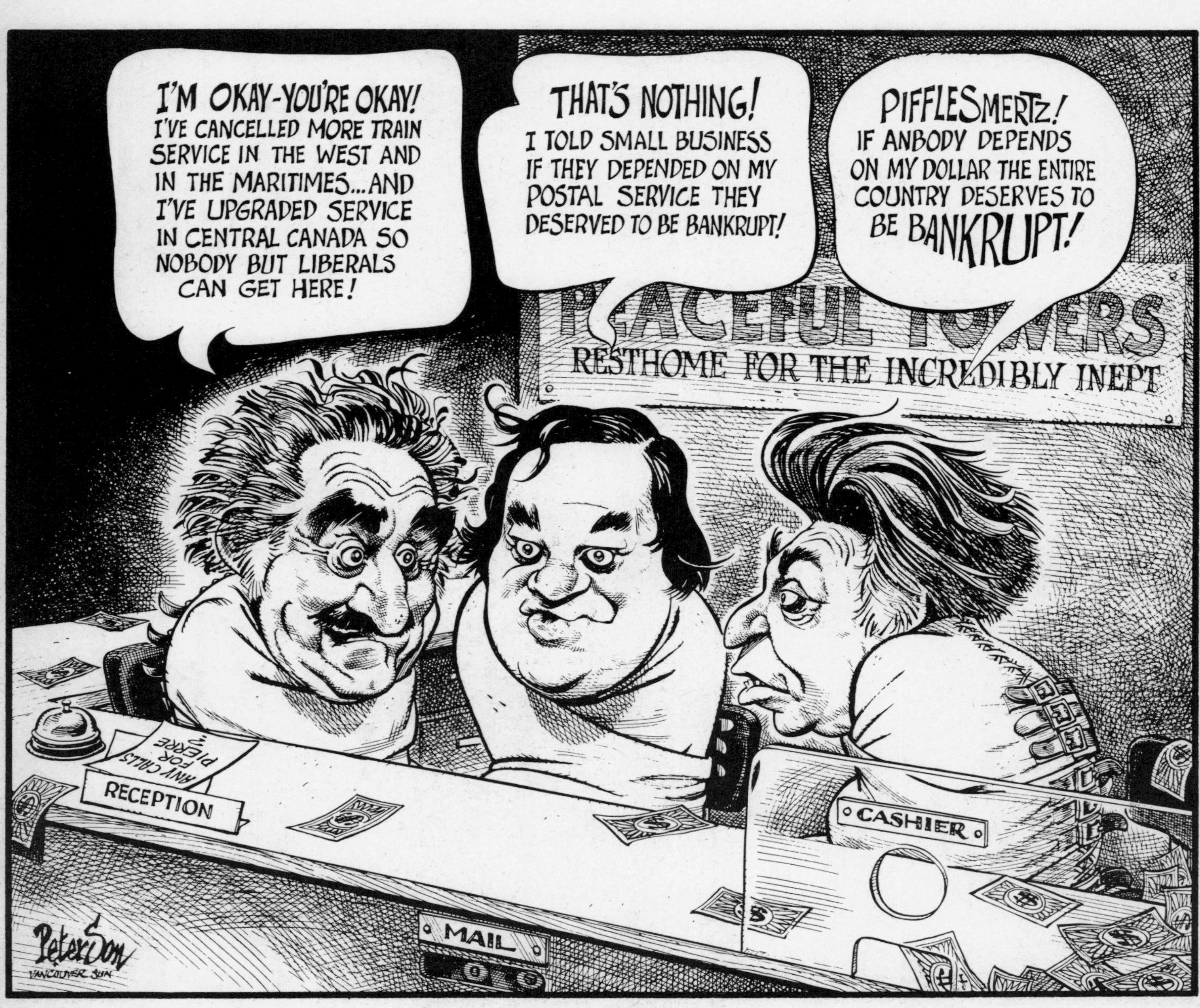

Running the Asylum

November 26, 1981

A Profit in his own land

December 3, 1981

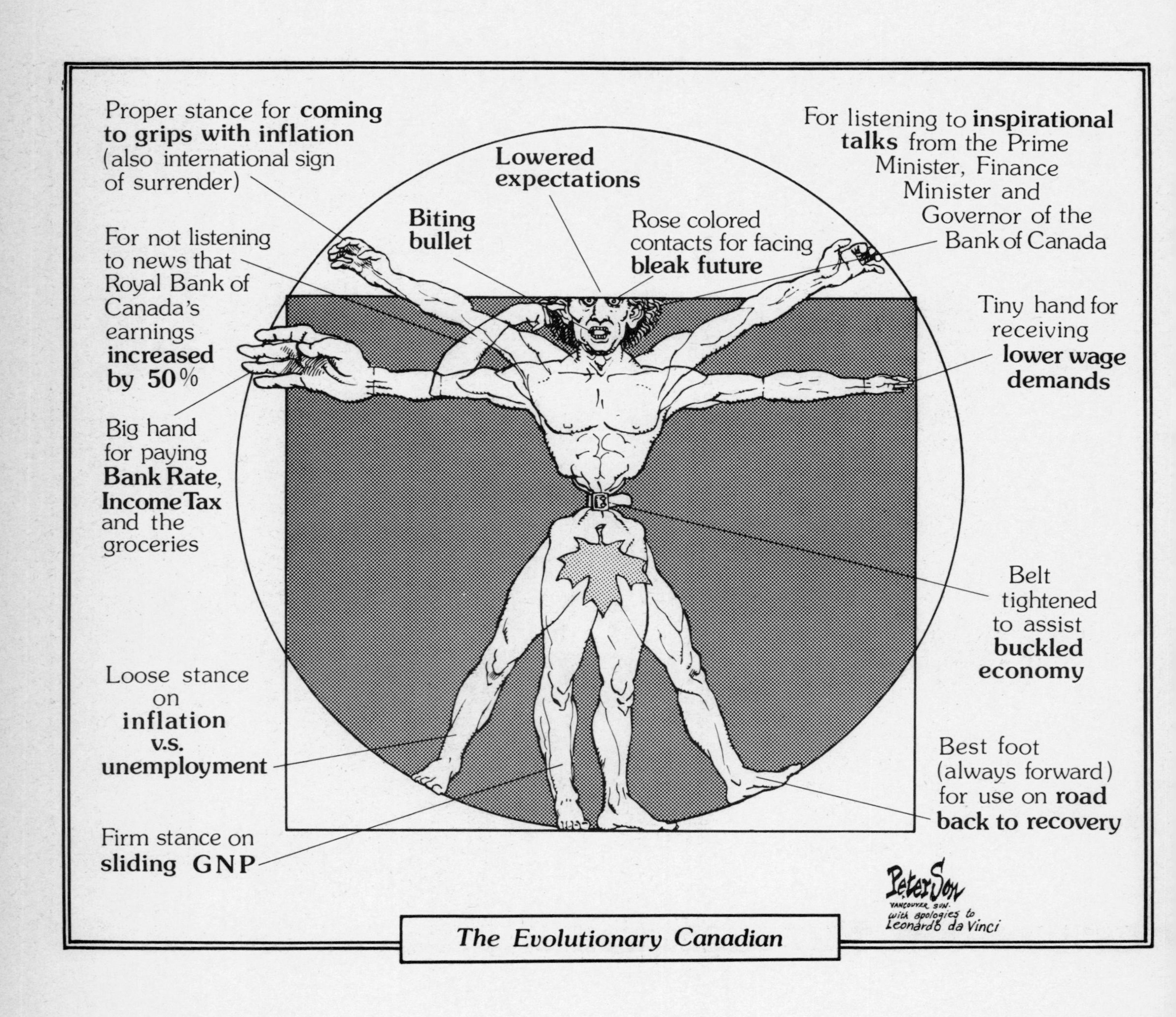

The Evolutionary Canadian

January 14, 1982

"Look at it this way — now you're one in a million . . ."

May 14, 1982

". . . patience Igor, we keep creating them until we get it right . . ."

June 23, 1982

". . . so, after the bankruptcy I thought . . . maybe Trudeau's right — maybe as a Western Liberal I ***have*** *been concentrating too much on business and not enough on social programs . . ."*

July 21, 1982

"That's amazing, Allan — can you get it to work the other way?"

September 8, 1982

"Don't you remember? We were standing in the breadline contemplating the soupe du jour . . . you'd just given the finger to the Great Canadian Jobless . . . then you started raving about committing more money in foreign aid to the needy of the world . . ."

January 27, 1983

". . . does it mention when the Depression begins?"

February 23, 1984

"Willie marches to a different drummer . . . he's a Liberal — but he's also unemployed . . . . "

January 26, 1981

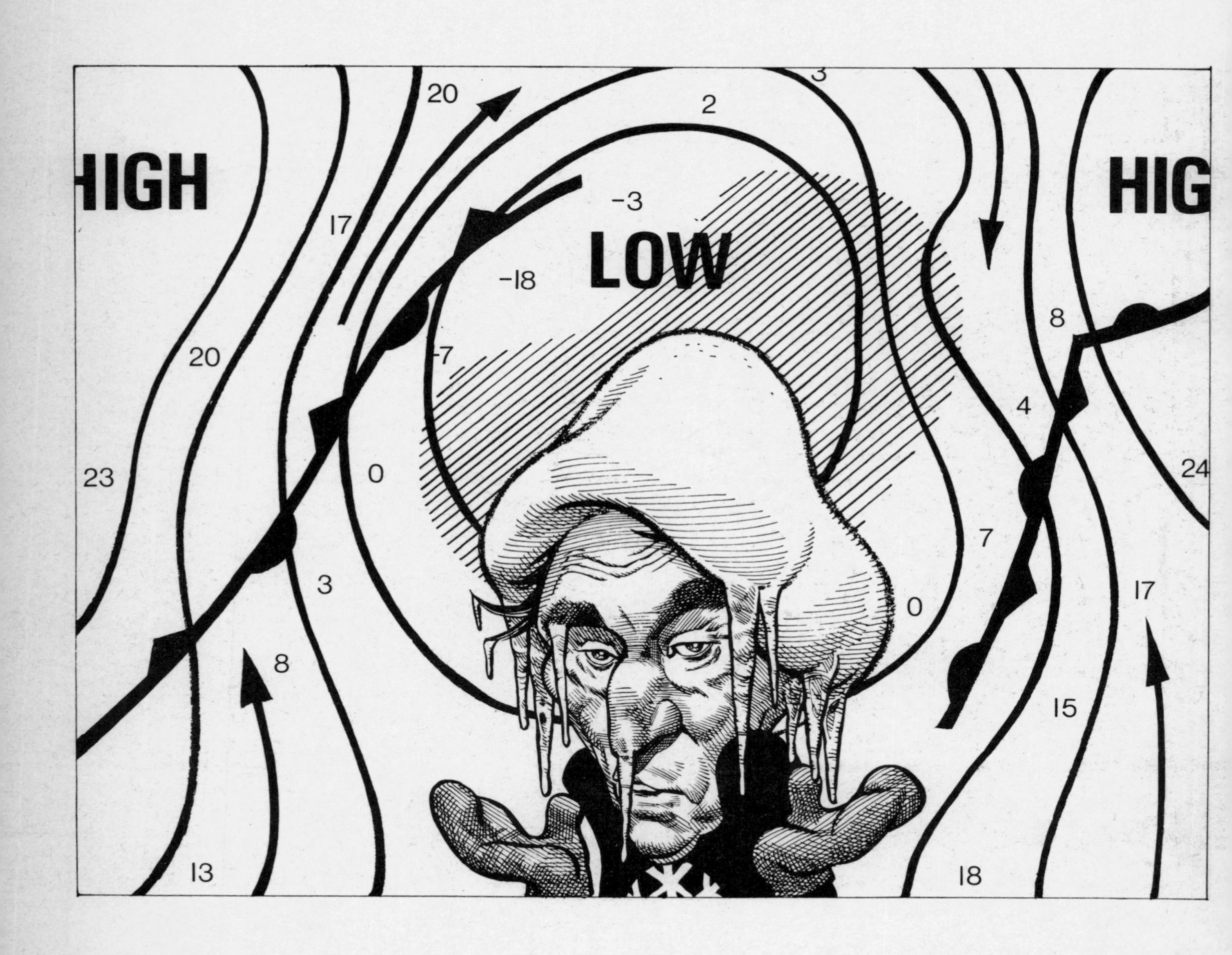

5

Kings 1, philosophers 0

ONLY FOUR YEARS after he had swept the nation's hearts and polls, Pierre Trudeau sat in a bedroom of Ottawa's Château Laurier Hotel on election night, calculating the knife-edge margin of the 1972 campaign that would retain him in office with a bedraggled minority. Turning to a sweating aide, he whispered: "I'll tell you one thing for certain: from now on, no more philosopher king."

Even in his inaugural campaign of '68, Trudeau had never really tried to paint himself as either philosopher or king, but the voters—looking for a rainbow at the end of a political downpour—thought they were electing a very special kind of man who would reject expediency and give Canada a new politics. Instead, Trudeau turned out to be only occasionally different from most middle-of-the-channel politicos who try to stay afloat on a sea of contradictory impulses; he sought shelter from each new electoral storm not in idealism but under the same umbrella that had protected most of his Liberal predecessors, a political credo they glorified with the term "functional pragmatism"—which really was little more than rampant opportunism.

When he first materialized on the national political scene, Trudeau attempted to toss off his reasons for running with such lines as, "I want to see where my ideas lead . . ." Nobody listened. I remember in particular one explanation he tried to deliver in Winnipeg on May 23, 1968, to a screeching passle of teeny-boppers and their parents: "I do not feel myself bound by any doctrines or rigid approaches," he intoned. "I am a pragmatist . . ." His unthinking, unhearing audience hollered in response: "You tell 'em, Pierre-baby."

A year later, in the calmer environs of a Liberal policy conference at Harrison Hot Springs, he tried again, this time reducing the process of governing to an almost mechanical formula: "We are like the pilots of a supersonic airplane," Trudeau explained. "By the time an airport comes into the pilot's field of vision, it is too late to begin the landing procedure. Such planes must be navigated by radar. A political party, in formulating policy, can act as society's radar . . . As members of a political party we should be thinking not only of the type of goals we wish to achieve in our society but of their relative importance, and of the best means of achieving them within a reasonable time." At that point, Canadian voters could still find whatever ideology suited them in their quixotic new prime minister—the progressive (as sponsor of some fairly radical reforms to the Criminal Code, for example) or the reactionary (in proclaiming a $120 limit on the two percent social development tax in his first budget).

There was nothing sinister in Trudeau's approach—simply a perpetuation of the good old Liberal ethic which holds that the chief function of the party is to stay in power by defining and refining bureaucratic initiatives. Out of Trudeau's essentially managerial approach came the feeling that he viewed the most serious of social problems in terms of efficiently handling their fallout, instead of attempting to resolve the unequal distribution of wealth that had caused them. This created what Charles Abrams, the American housing expert, once described as "socialism for the rich and capitalism for the poor"—an approach to governing that satisfied neither group.

As Trudeau reached for the ideal balance (occupying the political centre while moving simultaneously to the left and right), his government lost its vital intellectual core. This brought him dangerously close to fulfilling the prescription for political longevity attributed to Louis St. Laurent by the late Senator Maurice Lamontagne, who at one time worked in St. Laurent's office: "Because it is more and more impossible to keep all the people equally satisfied, we have to try to keep them equally *dis*satisfied," the P.M. had explained to his young assistant. That risky prescription would eventually defeat St. Laurent, and it almost did the same for Trudeau.

The legions of academic enthusiasts who enlisted early in the Trudeau crusade and organized campus clubs on his behalf were not misguided in viewing him as the first Canadian prime minister who had gone into politics with a recognizable set of beliefs, but his wasn't the progressive ideology they imagined they were supporting. Also, he faced the insoluble dilemma of every professor who dares enter the political arena: the intellectual seeks truth, the politician power, and the twin quests operate in separate orbits.

Trudeau and most of his ministers qualified as the Canadian equivalent of Whigs, a British political movement described by A.R.M. Lower, the Queen's University historian, as "people who in general were on the side of righteousness, took a benevolent attitude toward it, but felt no urge to advance interests other than their own or those with which they identified."

Trudeau saw himself as belonging in the tradition of Jean-Paul Sartre, the existentialist French philosopher who claimed that each individual is what he makes of himself—that "man invents himself through exercising his freedom of choice." This was a magic notion to the prime minister, especially during his early years in power, when he became familiar with the mystical entity of Canada for the first time and responded through authentic political acts to what he felt and saw. He imagined he could create a workable political credo by revealing the character of the nation to itself.

In the subsequent process of travel and observation, he realized what all perceptive Canadian prime ministers have come to know: that the country is just too big and much too diverse to be effectively governed; that even the man who occupies the nation's highest political office is there not to seek historical vindication but merely to preside over the choice of available options. Trudeau initially thought that the ideal way to govern would be to draw from his countrymen accurate soundings of what they really wanted, by presenting them with the facts and then asking them to back relevant policies. This is what his early push for "participatory democracy" was all about and, even if it failed, the attempt was a brave one. In an interview shortly after gaining office, he told me:

> We need to tell the people, 'Okay—if you want to have portable fridges on the beaches and portable television sets and so on, that's fine, but maybe we can't swim in the water because it's polluted. But if we want clean water, we'll have to pay higher taxes, which means we don't have our portable television sets . . .' Now what will people choose? Perhaps they'll choose television sets. But at least they won't say then that the government can't do anything about pollution. They'll say I'm suggesting we have to explain this to people. Explain that they must have choices. . . . It's a sense of helplessness which destroys society. It's the feeling that everything is out of control. But government can't really solve the problems by itself. . . . What preserves free societies is the facing of difficulties by all its citizens.

That was sound theory, but listening to what voters want can convey strange messages to a politician's inner ear. The citizen coalitions that make the most noise are not necessarily the most representative, and Trudeau had fun quoting Sir Rodmond Roblin, a former premier of Manitoba who complained in 1912 that he was "opposed by all the short-haired women and long-haired men in the province."

The reason there was such confusion about Trudeau's ideology was because of its original roots in parlor-pink socialism. "Trudeau was a man of the economic left," concluded Michael Walker, head of Vancouver's right-wing Fraser Institute. Such knee-jerk reactions were based mainly on Trudeau's essay, "Economic Rights," published in a 1962 edition of the *McGill Law Journal*: "Economic reform is impossible," he proclaimed at the time,

> so long as legislators, lawyers and businessmen cling to economic concepts which were conceived for another age. The liberal idea of property helped to emancipate the bourgeoisie, but it is now hampering the march toward economic democracy. The ancient values of private property have been carried over into the age of corporate wealth. As a result, our laws and our thinking recognize as proprietors of an enterprise men who today hold a few shares which they will sell tomorrow on the stock market, whereas workers who may have invested the better part of their lives and of their hopes in a job have no proprietary right to that job, and may be expropriated from it *without compensation* whenever a strike or lock-out occurs, whenever they grow old, or whenever Capital decides to disinvest. That same erroneous concept of property has erected a wall of prejudice against reform, and a wall of money against democratic control. As a consequence, powerful financial interests, monopolies and cartels are in a position to plan large sectors of the national economy for the profit of the few, rather than for the welfare of all. Whereas any serious planning by the State, democratically controlled, is dismissed as a step toward Bolshevism.

Not that revolutionary a doctrine—but it did call for the kind of class warfare being promoted by the CCF and, later, the NDP. Despite this and some of his similar proclamations in *Cité Libre*, Trudeau was a socialist less by persuasion than by virtue of the fact that it seemed like a handy institutionalized way to rebel in the Quebec where he was growing up. In 1965, when Lester Pearson enlisted him in the Liberal Party, Trudeau openly gave up his socialism and described his reasons in the foreword to *Federalism and the French Canadians*: "In joining the Liberals, I turned my back on the socialist party for which I had campaigned at a time when Quebec considered socialism to be treason and heresy; but I had no regrets because by then—in 1965—most of its Quebec followers were in fact exchanging socialism for nationalism. . . ."

Trudeau's loathing of nationalism, which he called "as obsolete as the divine right of kings," was a recurring theme in his early writings. He supported instead a concept he labelled "multinationalism" and praised Canada which, by accident of history, has become one of the world's few multinational states. His definition of nationalism seemed perilously close to its Nazi variety of the 1930s and 1940s. Though he vilified states that tried to dominate individuals or downgrade ethnic and religious groups, he was defining nationalism almost as racism. When I tried to place the notion in its Canadian context and asked him during a 1976 chat whether he thought there could be such a thing as defensive nationalism (which would allow Canada, for example, to protect its culture from the Americans), he replied: "You can call it 'defensive nationalism' if you want, just as in *Alice in Wonderland*. But for me, I'm afraid the word 'nationalism,' though it applies to cultural nationalism too, is very often a vehicle of the ruling classes to transfer wealth to themselves. . . ."

In the one great ideological turnabout of his years in office, Trudeau (briefly) donned a nationalist coat after his 1979 defeat. This conversion was mainly the work of Keith Davey, Jim Coutts, Marc Lalonde and Lloyd and Tom Axworthy. Heather Robertson decried the process in *Today* magazine: "The Liberal Party of Canada, the party of Reciprocity, Free Trade and Internationalism transformed itself into the champion of Canadian nationalism. Prominent Liberals everywhere now proclaim themselves to be nationalists with the shy, confessional courage of alcoholics who've just joined AA."

From this new policy thrust came the determination to "bash the Brits" into patriating the constitution; the National Energy Program, which succeeded in significantly raising Canadian ownership of the oil and gas industry; the made-in-Canada oil price that was lower than the world price; the buying spree of foreign-owned petroleum companies by Petro-Canada and the Canada Development Corporation; and the electoral victory of February 1980.

Then came the Great Recession, and Trudeau's nationalism faded into the background.

Trudeau's impatience with the parliamentary process never matched his contempt for nationalism, but it was much more public. He could rise to individual occasions (such as Leader's days, or budget debates or soliloquies on foreign affairs) but, most of the time, he regarded the House of Commons as a necessary evil. Front row centre, he sounded alternately bored and amused, trying to keep himself awake. He'd turn aside Opposition queries with quips, non sequiturs, historical allusions and the occasional expletive. Once in a long while he would come to life—and, when his intellect was roused, could be deadly with sloppy questioners. Most of the time he slouched through the sittings, following Orders of the Day with about as much interest as a bookie hearing last week's race results. Whatever argument some hapless Tory or New Democrat was making, chances were that Trudeau had already heard a similar view put more lucidly by members of his own inner circle, so that little really surprised or fascinated him and few parliamentary issues caught his attention.

Yet if he chose, he could be devastating. When nothing much was happening one hazy Ottawa summer day, Trudeau, bored out of his skull, decided to have some fun with Robert Stanfield, the former Nova Scotia premier, who was by then leader of the Conservative Party. "I really tend to forget," he gently opened, laying his trap,

> that the Leader of the Opposition has been involved in politics for so long—I choose the word 'involved' deliberately; I would not want to use the word 'active' because it does not seem quite appropriate—that he can continue to talk in 1970 in Ottawa in the same terms and in the same tone as he employed ten years ago in Halifax. I wonder whether he will continue to display this magnificent stolidity throughout the next few years.
>
> If so, I am sure that the disappearance of the Progressive Conservative Party as a relevant element in Canadian life will then be guaranteed. He may find that his party platform is replaced by the well-known anarchist Dr. Marcuse, because the sum total of his speech this morning and his concluding words were really Marcusian in nature. He concluded that the only thing that mattered was to throw out the government. . . .

The Tories sat there, stunned and uncomprehending. Finally, John Lundrigan, a backbencher from Newfoundland, lurched to his feet and sarcastically commented: "Pretty smart, I'd say."

Trudeau's mastery of the Commons was demonstrated most effectively just before he resigned as leader when, upon flying in from Yuri Andropov's funeral and the meeting with Konstantin Chernenko, he found his colleagues under siege for having investigated Conservative leader Brian Mulroney's private financial affairs. In minutes Trudeau had rallied his front benchers for a counter-attack, pointing out quite accurately that loss of privacy was one major cost of the political life and that any party that didn't keep files on its opponents was nuts. That such a marginal issue could so thoroughly have rattled the stay-at-homes demonstrated how depleted Liberal ranks had become.

A faint Orwellian air hung over the nation's capital during the Trudeau Years, as the leader patrolled the ranks of his followers like an unblinking shark, primitive and threatening to any dissenters. For their part, most of his colleagues were quite content to let Trudeau handle parliamentary matters. They tried to copy his air of elegant disdain in the House, but rarely could carry it off.

Trudeau swept away what he privately called "the sloppiness of the Commons," so that new bills moved through the legislative process according to strict timetables; supply motions could no longer be blockaded, and Question Period became less of a free-for-all. He concentrated much time and energy trying to make the Parliamentary process run more smoothly because he genuinely believed that democracy would fail if it weren't efficient enough. In one talk we had on this subject, he became excited, asking the rhetorical question: "Why did Fascism arise in Italy, Naziism in Germany and Gaulism in France? Not because some political party exaggerated its powers and used Parliament to squash the Opposition, but because in these countries the judgment was made that Parliament couldn't settle the issues fast enough. In other words, Naziism, Fascism and Gaulism arose exactly for the reasons we're trying to correct by making Parliament more efficient."

The toughest discipline was applied within the Liberal caucus. Instead of remaining the open-ended debating society it had been under Lester Pearson, MPs were limited to talking less than three minutes each, and only if they had placed their names on the caucus chairman's list. "The average Liberal MP," complained Phil Givens, a former mayor of Toronto and the first of a dozen Liberal backbenchers who quit in disgust, "is as useless as teats on a bull."

The average Liberal cabinet minister may not have felt quite so useless, but for most, life under Trudeau was an exercise in compliance and/or frustration.

Eric Kierans, the most enlightened intellect who ever sat in a Trudeau cabinet, once complained about the nature of cabinet deliberations. "It was like a papal procession. When the Pope steps from the altar at St. Peter's and walks down the aisle," he said, "the one thing you know is that he's going to get to the other end. You can argue and argue but, ultimately, the procession goes on its way. . . . In cabinet, you were always listened to with great respect, but nothing would ever happen. The other ministers would hear you out and then go back to their departments and do what the Establishment boys told them in the first place." Other ministers were even less flattering. Mitchell Sharp, thoroughly imbued with the Ottawa mystique, commented: "We plan and plan, but we don't do anything much. Cabinet has become an academic seminar."

Trudeau's approach to cabinet was more presidential than prime ministerial. He would lecture at length about how essential "countervailing forces" were to the welfare of the democratic state and about the intrinsic value of "the collegial decision-making process." But when it came to the exercise of power, the reality had little to do with the theory. He ran the shop, along with Michael Pitfield at the Privy Council office and the partisans who overflowed the PMO.

This was very different from the Pearson and Diefenbaker administrations in which individual ministers operated nigh-independent fiefdoms. Under Trudeau, every cabinet member's legislative and policy suggestions had to be submitted to the East Block deep-thinkers, who would then decide if and when the proposals would be put on the cabinet agenda. Authority was dispersed among half a dozen committees, with the thirteen-member Priorities and Planning Committee acting as the key group. The only way a minister could get any committee decision reversed by full cabinet was to notify the Privy Council office forty-eight hours ahead of time, giving good reasons for his or her objections. This was such an intimidating and cumbersome process that few ministers bothered, particularly since they were aware that any minister who was less than utterly prepared would be cut to ribbons.

The cabinet's most serious problem, however, was lack of continuity. Trudeau expressed dissatisfaction with his colleagues by repeatedly switching their portfolios. Only three men (Jean-Luc Pépin, Jean Chrétien and Allan MacEachen) survived as ministers throughout the Trudeau years. Most portfolios suffered from the game of musical chairs the PM insisted on playing; there were, for example, eleven ministers of Revenue during his term, ten ministers of Consumer and Corporate Affairs, and eight of National Defence.

In his many cabinet shuffles, Trudeau became stage director as well as principal actor, so that he was able not only to project his personal prerogative, but to impose on the public mind the scenario of each event. The dramatic resignation of Deputy Prime Minister Paul Hellyer, for instance, which ought to have shaken the administration, was fobbed off as being due to his misreading of the constitution. Hellyer vanished, leaving hardly a ripple to show he had ever existed. There was a kind of post-shuffle pecking order among departing ministers, depending on their loyalty to the Trudeau colors, and the treatment dispensed reflected this. Barney Danson, for example, who never wavered in his faith, was named to a pleasant diplomatic sinecure; Judd Buchanan, whose transgression was to suggest in 1979 that Trudeau's time as leader was over, was offered nothing.

If lack of continuity was the cabinet's most serious problem, its most serious weakness—which ultimately caused Trudeau more political grief than anything else—was the absence of a strong lieutenant from English Canada. Successful Canadian prime ministers have always sought to create a concurrent cabinet majority by sharing their powers with a senior colleague from the other founding culture. Trudeau did not, and paid dearly for it.

Around the cabinet table, Trudeau's ministers were reduced to a league of awed men and women, not so much afraid to challenge his views as uncertain of their own in the face of his intellectual agility and strength of purpose. Somehow, the political chemistry never jelled. An administration that was to have been delicately programmed and exquisitely managed became instead a troupe of ambitious but obedient pranksters who would have been the pride of the social director on the *Titanic*.

6

His strength was as the strength of ten

Trudeau and the premiers had a perfect non-working relationship; on a rare good day, they might agree to disagree.

February 20, 1980

". . . and I am reminded that while we face the threat of separatism in Quebec, we must not turn our backs on the alienation of the West . . . ."

July 9, 1973

Parlez vous Western Canadian?

April 8, 1975

The National Sport

November 20, 1976

May 24, 1977

"Looks like we'll have to escalate the July 1st fireworks order, Barney — better make it 100 gross skyrockets, 10,000 pinwheels, 30,000 Roman candles and . . . what the hell, 375 short-range pre-emptive strike missiles just in case . . . "

October 3, 1977

The Canadianese Twins

November 28, 1977

Funny cigarettes

January 9, 1978

"I don't care what Mackenzie King says, Charles, by the time they get to read MY diaries we'll have won the referendum."

February 18, 1978

February 25, 1978

June 10, 1978

February 7, 1980

"Only in Eastern Canada, you say . . ."

April 18, 1980

The enemy within

May 22, 1980

"Now let's find out what they'll swallow . . . ."

May 29, 1980

"Remember the rule: half the oil we expected from Mexico at world price means all the oil we expect from Alberta at half the world price."

May 30, 1980

WE HAVE SEEN THE ENEMY AND THEY IS PREMIER PECKFORD OF NEWFOUNDLAND
...AND THEY IS MIGHTY SUSPISHUS OF OL' PETE LOUGHEED AN' BILLY BENNETT TOO!
SPIRIT OF ENOOED FEDERALISM
Peterson
VANCOUVER SUN
WITH APOLOGIES TO WALT KELLY AND 'POGO'

June 6, 1980

"The good cop/bad cop technique of dealing with the premiers is working, but come on you guys . . . ONE of us has to be the good cop."

July 4, 1980

"Whatever you do, don't try to go west of the Winnipeg city limits . . . ."

July 16, 1980

"At least they're fuel-efficient — they're boiling the oil with natural gas . . . "

July 31, 1980

"In the interest of national stability, of course, you get the barrel free."

August 28, 1980

"As a matter of fact the prime minister is going over your constitutional proposals right now . . . ."

September 17, 1980

"It's either a new get-tough policy with the provinces, a patriation costume party, or they've been watching too much Shogun during caucus . . ."

October 30, 1980

"So, you know, chances of Western separatism are absolutely nil and inexistent." PIERRE TRUDEAU, OCTOBER 23, 1980

"That's odd — he's never listened to us before . . . "

October 15, 1981

I put a position on the table and Premier Bennett is going to talk to his fellow premiers and he [Bennett] put a position on the table and I'll think about it.

— Pierre Trudeau, Oct. 14, 1981

Immaculate Western Conception

March 3, 1982

NO MORE MR. NICE GUY! SINCE WE CAN'T PLEASE THE PROVINCES WE NO LONGER TRY! THAT'S THE NEW FEDERALISM!
... SHEESH, A FEDERAL SEPARATIST!
GRIT CITY AC
GIVE
PeterSon
VANCOUVER SUN

August 5, 1983

"We must put an end to this inter-empire fed-bashing. Have my love letters to the premiers been received? Good . . . now stand by to nuke 'em with the cruise just in case . . . . "

7

How the West was lost

ARISTOTLE, who would have savored Pierre Trudeau's judicious approach to government, decreed that the boundaries of a Greek town should extend only to the limits of the sound of a cry for help at its centre. That admonition, translated into its modern Canadian context, became one of the dominant tenets of the Trudeau administration: he tried to govern Canada by governing Parliament Hill. But Canada—stretching through half a dozen time zones and covering a twelfth of the earth's surface—could not be administered in the same gentle way as a city-state.

Trudeau and his entourage acted as if they believed the country could be divided into three self-contained protectorates: Lower Canada (Quebec), Upper Canada (Ontario) and Outer Canada (Everything Else). Trudeau catered to Lower Canada, ruled Upper Canada and ignored Outer Canada, both East and West. While flailing away at the Tories for being unresponsive to the aspirations of Quebec, he was equally insensitive to the needs of the Canada that lay west of Toronto, east of Quebec City, or northward into the Arctic.

Under Trudeau's predecessor, Lester Pearson, there had evolved a sense of Western alienation that had netted him only six of the 192 Prairie seats available in four election campaigns. But when Trudeau burst on the scene, Liberal fortunes in the West were transformed. Dr. Pat McGeer, then a Liberal member of the British Columbia legislature and a delegate to the 1968 convention, explained the phenomenon: "For the West, where the French are feared because they are unknown, Trudeau lives and breathes the answer to the Quebec problem. People can transfer their worries about national unity to him. In his very person, he gives us all a feeling that the second culture in Canada is precious to preserve." In that first campaign, the West responded to the Trudeau magic, electing twenty-seven

Liberals and creating a new national majority. At the time, the Liberals were still powerful in the West's four provincial legislatures, with fifty-seven MLAs firmly in place.

Trudeau's first cabinet included six Western ministers, but Ottawa, captivated by French Canada's Renaissance, quickly lost interest in the West's problems. The prime minister confined his attempts to gain political favor among the twelve million Canadians who live west of Toronto's Humber River to such antics as putting on a cowboy hat occasionally, making nasty quips to Saskatchewan grain growers and staging grandiloquent gabfests such as the Western Economic Opportunities Conference in July 1973, which promised much and accomplished nothing.

In a strict accounting sense (their 1979 defeat being the exception), the Liberals didn't need Western votes to retain power—a fact painfully brought home on four out of five election nights as Knowlton Nash announced, long before the time-zone difference had closed Western polling booths: "It's all over. The Liberal government has been re-elected!" Sheer mathematics also dictated that Metropolitan Toronto, that paunchy defender of the status quo, deserved all the political attention it could get; its twenty-eight seats encompassed seven more than all of Alberta.

But politics in Canada (or Canada itself, for that matter) can never be based on mathematics alone. Throughout most of the twentieth century, the Liberal Party had maintained its national dominance by playing off two or three regions of the country against the rest—though they carefully masqueraded this divide-and-rule strategy as a commitment to "national unity." Under Sir Wilfrid Laurier and Mackenzie King, Quebec and much of the West (particularly Manitoba and Saskatchewan) were aligned against Tory Ontario. Under Pearson, Quebec and Ontario joined forces against the growing economic clout of the West, so that only in the Atlantic region did both traditional parties remain in genuine competition.

To keep their electoral machine primed, the Liberals depended on their provincial counterparts, and it was always the first sign of an impending federal debacle when that support vanished. (Just before their 1930 defeat, the Liberals had retained power in just one province—Quebec—and in 1957, when John Diefenbaker swept the country, only Joey Smallwood's eccentric administration in Newfoundland still flew the Liberal banner. By the end of the Trudeau Years, not a single Liberal government survived outside Ottawa itself and there was only one Liberal MLA in any of the four Western legislatures.)

Trudeau's alienation of the West had much to do with the inability of his ministers and advisors to comprehend how that dynamic sector of the country was changing. Until the late 1950s, national attention had been focused on the Prairies and British Columbia by the discoveries of petroleum and gas reserves, the carving out of an aluminum kingdom at Kitimat, the building of the Trans-Canada pipeline, the emergence of giant forest product complexes and the discoveries of rich new mineral deposits. But during the 1960s and 1970s, national concerns shifted to Ontario, where the country's industrial future was being molded, and to Quebec, where the struggle for national unity was being fought. The West began to feel a deepening sense of isolation from the centres of national decision-making. The resultant frustration was made worse by the fact that the West no longer had its own parties of political protest through which it could funnel its frustrations and needs. All the indigenous Western political movements (such as the federal wing of the Social Credit, the Progressive Party, the United Farmers of Alberta) had either vanished or, like the CCF, had been taken over by others. The Prairies had lived for half a century in a state of philosophical contradiction. Westerners took inordinate pride in individualism, free enterprise and the undisturbed market. Yet no other region in the country remained as deeply committed to the notions of governmental responsibility, price supports and government subsidies.

The Trudeau Liberals, at least in their early years, thought that all they had to do was sell piles of wheat to keep the West happy, or at least quiet. But even for farmers, this marked only the beginning of their concerns. What few Ottawa politicians appreciated was that Westerners working the land had long ago turned away from the frontier ethic. The pervasive impact of television and travel had given them feelings and ambitions not dissimilar from those of the cubicled dudes in the urban East.

This was the root of the matter: that Westerners were striving for precisely the same goals as Quebeckers—more say about their individual and collective destinies. What really worried them was that most of their labors went into producing resources destined for external markets over which they had no control. That was why the West needed champions (not just wheat salesmen) inside the larger circles of power in Ottawa. When they talked about *control*, Westerners really meant getting away from the stifling influence of the commercial, industrial and transportation mega-interests of Eastern Canada—from those anxious to turn the West into an exploitable hinterland.

Theirs was a justified anger, but Trudeau never understood its basis and so did little to defuse it.

What really happened during the Trudeau Years was that the very nature of Canada—a country agonizingly settled and developed along an east-west axis—swung around yet again to a north-south direction. Nearly everything that moved—air traffic, long-distance calls and computer hookups, trade, taste, ideas and ambitions—started to flow "up and down," rather than *across* the continent. The feds, who for generations had been hypnotized by the Ottawa-Montreal-Toronto axis (or if they were really daring, the Washington-New York-Boston axis), still regarded Canada as an extension of Donald Creighton's "Empire of the St. Lawrence." For example, their concept of British Columbia, if they thought of it at all, was that of a troublesome outpost on a distant second shore. Harry J. Boyle, the imaginative chairman of the CRTC, recognized the syndrome. He once aptly described the Trudeau mandarins as "always running around scared that somebody was going to dump tea into Vancouver Harbor."

That was bad enough, but most Liberals didn't even take into account the very obvious changes that were taking place in the economy of the Prairies. Even in Saskatchewan, the nation's so-called breadbasket, farming was providing less than half the gross provincial product by the mid-1960s. The provincial economy became more broadly based, with petroleum, potash, pulp and power displacing agriculture as the main sources of income. "Ears that were deaf to the urgency of developing a northern oil and gas strategy and the construction of a national power grid in the 1950s and 1960s," remarked Roy Faibish, an astute political thinker, "suddenly awakened in the late 1970s as we entered the 1980s bereft of energy, imagination and new ideas." The OPEC crisis of the early 1970s demonstrated how dependent Canada had become on its energy sources, and fully three-quarters of them were located west of the Lakehead.

Except for some inspired but very late politicking by Senator Jack Austin in British Columbia, the Trudeauites let half the country go—by default. "Liberal workers deserted the party en masse," noted Don Baird, the *Edmonton Journal*'s political columnist. "They left behind a servile collection of hacks who do their chores in return for favors, but have no rapport with the voters. Often, they don't even want their candidates to win because Liberal MPs would threaten their influence." With few exceptions, the Liberal candidates fielded by the Party were city slickers in overalls and heavy-handers with Massey-Ferguson franchises. They may have been machine-tooled to the specifications of their Ottawa-based patrons, but they did nothing to help the Liberals' policies span the Prairies or scale the Rockies.

Pierre Trudeau's legacy to the West was encapsuled in his offhand putdown to Saskatchewan farmers ("Why should I sell your wheat?") and his jabbing finger salute at Salmon Arm.

No matter what was happening in the West, the country's intelligentsia, with Trudeau in the vanguard, was fixated on Quebec as the focus of change. After all, trying to remedy the subservient status of the French language and culture in Canada was the main reason for Pierre Trudeau's interest in public policy. His lifelong crusade was based on the belief that, without a vibrant Quebec, "Canada wouldn't have any heart and Canadian life would cease." It proved difficult enough to convince French Canadians, seized by a frenzy of nationalism, that their best chance of surviving as a proud, autonomous society was through a firm alliance with the larger powers of the Canadian nation—but persuading Canada's English-speaking majority that Quebec should be granted special concessions proved a far tougher task. Many of the voters in the West, the Maritimes and rural Ontario who had so enthusiastically backed Trudeau in 1968 did so because they thought he would use his political clout to "put Quebec in its place."

Trudeau's success in heading off a major confrontation, his ability to accommodate Quebec's aspirations within Confederation, however temporarily, was his administration's greatest triumph. Few other major nationalist movements have been stopped short of achieving independence without the use of force, war or revolution.

Typically, it took an outsider to commemorate the PM's impressive achievement. "When Trudeau came to power in 1968," wrote Gwynne Dyer, the London-based commentator, "Canada was very close to breaking up. Another ten years on the same course, without the policies that Trudeau forced on a largely unwilling country, and Canada would have been gone. The wave of nationalist emotion which has brought a separatist provincial government to power in Quebec would probably have carried French Canada to independence by now without Trudeau's intervention. . . . In one or two decades' time, Canadians will probably recognize him as the greatest man Canada has produced. There might not now be a Canada without him."

"Language rights" was the instrument Trudeau used to open up the rest of the country to Quebec. In 1969, he hammered through an Official Languages Act which permitted Quebeckers to speak French with federal officials across the country. He appointed francophones to every major economic portfolio, including Finance, and proved conclusively that they were at least no worse than their anglophone predecessors. Although New Brunswick became the only officially bilingual province and the issue in Manitoba will continue to preoccupy Trudeau's successor, bilingualism had become an irreversible reality by the end of Trudeau's term.

This relatively orderly process was interrupted by the events of October 1970, when two armed men abruptly kidnapped British Trade Commissioner James Cross from his Montreal home. These and other acts of terror, particularly the brutal murder of Quebec Labor Minister Pierre Laporte, prompted Trudeau to call out the armed forces and invoke the War Measures Act, which Canada had never before applied in peacetime. Its provisions, which allowed police to search and arrest without warrants, jail without charge, and hold without bail, seemed to go against everything Trudeau believed. Countless times he had reiterated that people can be ruled only insofar as they agree to obey—yet in this instance, he was willing to brush aside accusations that he was violating basic human rights. "It's more important to maintain law and order," he commented, "than to worry about those whose knees tremble at the sight of the army." When a reporter asked how far he would go in support of law and order, Trudeau delivered perhaps his most famous challenge: "Just watch me!"

After the troubles were largely over, I had a long talk with Trudeau about the War Measures Act and its imposition; what I remember most about that session was his reaction when I suggested that, if he had not gone into politics, but had stayed as a lecturer at the University of Montreal pursuing his reform causes, he would surely have been arrested and had his books seized in the October 1970 police roundup. "Let me answer you in theory," he replied. "If I had been on the side of those who were challenging the authority of the duly elected representatives—then I bloody well would have deserved to be in the risk of being arrested. You can't have anarchy without somebody getting a boot in the ass at the hands of the duly elected government. So, if I'd been on the side of the anarchists, I hope I would have been mature enough to say, 'Well, I personally didn't deserve it, but I can understand the state not lying down and letting the anarchists take over' . . ."

Trudeau's strong reaction helped fan separatism in Quebec so that, six years later, René Lévesque's Parti Québécois triumphed over the corrupt Bourassa regime to claim power—and a mandate to withdraw from Confederation. Lévesque eventually translated his cause into a referendum, held in the spring of 1980. The burden of the federalists' case was carried somewhat uneasily by provincial Liberal leader Claude Ryan, whose preference for special status within Confederation didn't tally with Trudeau's formula.

It was the prime minister's finest hour. His carefully planned speeches and appearances diffused the sovereignty issue and, at the same time, allowed him to enlist the rest of the country in his grand strategy of pushing through his constitutional reforms. When the federal side decisively won the referendum, Trudeau turned his attention to fashioning a new constitution. He had been waving this idea for years, like a leper's bell, at anyone who would listen. It would allow him to enshrine language rights; it would finally sever Canada's umbilical cord with Mother Britain.

Initially, eight of the ten provinces violently opposed the Trudeau initiative, but the Supreme Court eventually ruled that approval by a majority of the provinces was required only by custom, not by law. Through a series of intricate maneuvers, Trudeau obtained the blessing of every province except Quebec and on April 17, 1982, the Queen confirmed Canada's status as an independent nation—at last.

8

L'enfant de la patrie

If he ended up as only a footnote to history, that footnote would begin: "He was the man who brought home the Constitution . . ."

June 11, 1980

Constitutional Reform

October 4, 1976

"It's some sort of ritualistic club, I think . . . they meet frequently all over the country to reaffirm their colonial mentality . . ."

June 20, 1980

WESTMINSTER
TUCK SHOP
SPECIAL
TODAY
SH & CHIPS
British North America
Act
LONDON
ON $5.00
A DAY
Peterson
VANCOUVER SUN

June 26, 1980

...I WOULD CONSIDER RETIREMENT ONCE MY SON GETS HIS ACT TOGETHER.
I'M CONSIDERING THE SAME THING ONCE I GET THE BNA ACT TOGETHER...
EIIR
EIIR
Peterson
VANCOUVER SUN

July 23, 1980

"Think of it, children . . . your future and the destiny of Canada, it s traditions and heritage will be defined once and for all by the decisions of the learned leaders now bashing the hell out of each other behind these doors . . ."

August 15, 1980

"As we say in the advertising game, Spendly—let's run it up the flagpole and see if any provincial-minded, resource-hoarding, anti-federalist son-of-the-soil salutes ...."

September 3, 1980

Dr. Jekyll and Mr. Trudeau

Ball three, strike two, two out, bottom of the ninth . . .
and the bases are loaded.

October 9, 1980

"UNI, meaning me dealing with one policy; LATER, meaning the economy, unemployment, inflation, and everything else . . . and AL, meaning MacEachen, who will explain why we haven't done anything about . . . LATER . . . "

CONSTITUTION
FOUNDATIONS
PLANS
QUIK-DRI
CLOSURE
CEMENT
Peterson
VANCOUVER SUN

October 31, 1980

Hysteria and Oursteria

January 16, 1981

February 4, 1981

"My Fairly Responsive Lady"

March 25, 1981

Constitutional Seesaw

April 3, 1981

"Stand by with Plan C . . . "

April 9, 1981

BUS STOP
BYTOWN EXPRESS
WESTMINSTER
HAVE A NICE DAY
NDP
YOU JUST CAUGHT US IN TIME!
GO
VROOOM VROOOM!
BNA
BYTOWN EXPRESS
N.B.
ONTARIO
APPLES
ORANGES
WHEN DO YOU PLAN TO RE-TIRE?
Peterson
VANCOUVER SUN

May 20, 1981

HMMM... FLABBY ECONOMY, CHRONIC UNEMPLOYMENT, HIGH INTEREST RATE PRESSURE, FITS OF DEPRESSION...
YES, BUT WHAT A MARVELLOUS CONSTITUTION!
CANADA
PETERSON
VANCOUVER SUN

June 24, 1981

Superman Deux

September 17, 1981

"Davis, ask Hatfield if he can see any sign of the S.S. Constitution on the horizon . . . Davis? . . . Davis? . . . Hatfield . . . ?"

September 29, 1981

October 28, 1981

The MacPatriation Brothers

November 5, 1981

". . . two more years of active indecision . . . then we drop back and punt it into the stands and let the crowd referee . . . ."

November 25, 1981

"Well excuu-u-se me!"

December 4, 1981

February 12, 1982

"Ordinarily I wouldn't rush you but in these times of restraint in Canada we do have to decide between bread or circuses . . ."

April 15, 1982

9

Hello, cruel world

THE GREAT PEACE INITIATIVE that marked the hectic months before his exit left Trudeau-watchers wondering if, had he given himself more time and energy to pursue his great elusive chase, "something real" might have been accomplished. As it was, Trudeau's forays abroad were sporadic at best, and his imprint on world councils was that of a dilettante with unrealized potential.

National defence and foreign affairs were subjects too drowsy to lend themselves readily to Trudeau's wit, but he did his best. In August 1969, when he made his first dive aboard one of Canada's obsolescent submarines and was asked how he liked it, he clicked his heels, assumed his best U-boat-Kapitan pose and declared: "When I grow up, I want to be a submarine commander." In the summer of 1982, he adroitly encapsuled American-Canadian relations when he told a scholarly audience: "Our main exports to the United States are hockey players and cold fronts. Our main imports are baseball players and acid rain."

Trudeau's view of the world never varied very much from his days on *Cité Libre*, where he railed at "the anti-democratic reflexes of the spineless Liberal herd" for having accepted the nuclear-tipped Bomarcs on Canadian soil. In his 1963 attacks on Lester Pearson's pro-nuclear decision, Trudeau found himself in the paradoxical position of defending John Diefenbaker: "For a long time," he editorialized,

> it has been clear that the U.S.A. did not like Mr. Diefenbaker. From the beginning, he had proposed to strengthen the ties with the Commonwealth and decrease those with the U.S.A. . . . He had chosen an external affairs minister who loved peace more than he loved the Americans. He was selling wheat to China . . . traded with Cuba . . . Mr. Kennedy's hipsters could not tolerate this . . . The word was passed around: Diefenbaker must go. So it was easy for the Americans to give a helping hand to defeat a government already wavering since the first day after the elec-

> tion. The helping hand came from the Pentagon, and demanded that Mr. Pearson betray his party program, along with the idealism with which he was identified. Funds were plentiful. Gallup indicated that a pro-nuclear policy would not lose him the majority of electors. Power was within Mr. Pearson's reach—he had nothing to lose, except honor.

It said a lot about the generosity of Pearson's spirit that half a decade later he would manoeuvre events to make certain Trudeau would be chosen as his successor, and on June 19, 1968, good old Mike went to the wall for his former tormentor. "He is the man for today," he told a Liberal election rally. "He is the man for tomorrow. He is the man, who, if he gets a majority in the House of Commons, will help to hold his country together and help to move it forward in the right direction to a great future."

When he first assumed power, Trudeau repaid the favor by dissociating himself from the Pearson approach to world affairs. Canada, he declared, would henceforth stop trying to be "the helpful fixer," and would attempt instead to achieve well-defined national objectives in its external relations. This meant that Ottawa would no longer pretend that our contributions to international alliances could be camouflaged as the primary goal of foreign policy. Even here, Trudeau managed to transpose his longing for French rights into the world context. "If I didn't think we could create some form of a bilingual country," he told a hushed gathering of External Affairs officers, "I would no longer be interested in working in Ottawa."

He cut Canada's NATO contingent in half, and tried to win points by emphasizing the possibility of economic growth through more international trade. In American-Canadian relations, Trudeau made friends with Jimmy Carter and enemies with Ronald Reagan. He contributed many useful initiatives to the annual Commonwealth conferences, was early off the mark in recognizing mainland China and put into place some brave sovereignty declarations on our Arctic coastline. Most of all, he travelled: *anything* to get out of Ottawa.

"The Trudeau government," commented professors Adam Bromke and Kim Nossal of McMaster University, "got the worst of both worlds: it achieved none of the positive benefits of non-alignment, yet it lost respectability in the Western alliance. Canada remained tied to the U.S. economy. And in the second half of the 1970s, the dangers to world peace posed by the decline of East-West detente were compounded by the development of a new generation of military weaponry. The low priority given to foreign policy exacted a price in the long run: the slow evaporation of Canada's most potent resource in international politics—its influence. Nowhere was Ottawa's declining prestige in the world more starkly evident than in the prime minister's diplomatic finale—his peace initiative."

In that final crusade, Trudeau found himself back in a Pearsonian mode, trying to pump up Canada's credentials abroad and grabbing Brownie points wherever he could, even when it meant pretending that rhetorical homilies from Gustav Husak, the puppet dictator of Czechoslovakia, actually meant something.

At last, Trudeau discovered first hand the sad truth about Canada's world standing: that within our alliances we were regarded as a free-rider on the backs of the American taxpayers and as a client-state of the Pentagon. Trudeau underlined this attitude by admitting that, "Canada is in the extraordinarily fortunate position of not having to defend itself because we know darn well that the United States will defend us. They won't let a hostile nation take over Canada to wage war on the United States."

He followed up on this colonial pronouncement by reducing Canada's armed forces to joke proportions and listing national defence as his cabinet's fourteenth priority, just after price supports for hogs. What Trudeau forgot was that, in the disarmament sweepstakes, your clout is equivalent to what you throw into the pot. Since, under Trudeau, Canada became perhaps the only nation in world history to disarm itself unilaterally, he ended up zooming around the world to little avail, finding no takers for his grand ideas. Everyone supported his cause but no one joined it.

"The peace initiative," commented Gerald Wright, president of the Atlantic Council of Canada, a NATO support group, "was hatched almost overnight. It did not come out of long years of hard thought and expertise. On Trudeau's part, it never had a completely true ring. There were long periods when he had never given any attention to the subject at all." Trudeau discovered what our diplomats had known all along: that some of his domestic political foes may have been dangerous, but that world statesmen are deadly—especially when it comes to taking credit for helping to preserve our delicate planet. They were not about to share the glory with a new member of their club they could not yet take completely seriously.

Of all the many steps he took in a genuine effort to try to defuse world tensions, Trudeau's most incomprehensible, and most controversial, policy initiative was in agreeing to test the cruise missile for the Americans. To justify his actions, which flew in the face of his previous vehement opposition to having the nuclear-tipped Bomarc missiles stationed on Canadian soil, Trudeau trotted out the artificial arguments that this particular test of this specific missile over northern Alberta was required to meet Canada's commitments to NATO, and that its overflights could be used as a bargaining lever in prompting the Soviets to take disarmament more seriously.

None of these statements was true, and Trudeau must have known it. This was not the weapon being deployed in Europe (which was a ground-launched, not air-launched, cruise); the territory over which the NATO missiles would be travelling (to predetermined targets inside the Soviet Union) would supposedly be industrialized Europe and not land comparable to northern Alberta. The cruise had no logical connection with the weapons then under discussion at the Geneva disarmament talks. What Trudeau was agreeing to do, though he never admitted it, was to test over Canada a second-generation strategic weapon which, in the event of war, would be launched—not by NATO forces, but by U.S. Strategic Air Command bombers—directly across the North Pole at Soviet cities. That was why the tests over territory resembling the Russian tundra were so important. The real reason for allowing the cruise into Canada was as a trade-off, so that Trudeau could use the testing agreement to take the pressure from Washington and NATO off his government. He had been pressed for years, domestically and internationally, to spend some real money increasing the potential of Canada's *conventional* armed forces.

Thus we ended the Trudeau Years as an even more humble client-state of the Pentagon than before, denied the freedom of action so precious to countries more independent than ours.

10

The international dream

He didn't bestride the world like a colossus, but he did bestride the world — as often as he could.

December 2, 1983

"... er, some of the fans in the stands have asked me to ask you both to hold the noise down out here ..."

May 17, 1971

". . . and then the peasants, suffering from rising unemployment coupled with higher prices and unfair taxes . . . revolted . . ."

January 15, 1973

"Fillerup!"

February 24, 1975

Words to Live By

February 21, 1977

" . . . but then every time I mentioned separation he'd jump and shout ' The South has riz agin! ' . . . "

January 9, 1981

March 6, 1981

"For God's sake don't laugh — he hasn't appointed an ambassador to Canada yet . . ."

July 16, 1981

The Monster that Ate America

July 17, 1981

"Okay, okay — you can sit there until the others arrive and we can all decide where you're to be placed on the agenda . . ."

September 18, 1981

"Have I got screws for you . . . ."

September 24, 1981

Podnuhs

October 23, 1981

"I understand he was chosen co-chairman because of his charm, spirit of co-operation and willingness to negotiate with anyone other than a provincial premier . . ."

October 30, 1981

"Frankly, Pierre, not only are we annoyed that there's too much Canadian investment in American industry — we're really hacked that there's too much Canadian investment in Canadian industry . . ."

". . . they're led by an enigmatic mystic, of course . . . owns only one Mercedes . . . "

March 26, 1982

"You have nothing to fear but FIRA itself."

June 17, 1982

January 5, 1983

February 9, 1983

February 16, 1983

"As far as I'm concerned, Pierre, you can still be a hewer of wood as long as you're a guider of missiles . . . "

February 18, 1983

"Damned if I know how they developed it, but I understand its memory system had to be specifically approved by the Canadian cabinet . . . "

March 24, 1983

"I can safely say Vice-President Bush was impressed when I assured him Canada supports President Reagan's Zero Option policy to such an extent that we'd already applied it to the Canadian Maritime forces."

May 18, 1983

"Ronnie baby, nobody's saying you're the Darth Vader of the '80s . . . it's just that . . . if you could lighten up a bit when you exhale . . . ."

October 6, 1983

"Nasty old bloodstains got you down, Yuri? Then try all-new Cold War Cool, with the miracle ingredient P.E.T. which turns murderous superpower confrontations into simple 'tragic accidents' . . . !"

November 3, 1983

". . . as a result of direct secret talks with Mr. Trudeau regarding his quest for world peace, Miss Streisand has declared areas of the Bronx, Brooklyn, and Beverly Hills as Nuclear Free Zones. . . ."

November 16, 1983

". . . are you sure this is how Lester Pearson won his Nobel Peace Prize . . . ?"

December 8, 1983

"So I said to Ronnie, nuclear payload or not, I understand these babies are supposed to seek out the Russians and get an immediate response from Andropov . . ."

December 15, 1983

Pentagon Pipsqueak Oil

January 19, 1984

"Okay, okay — have it your way . . . when I've achieved World Peace I'll return to drawing Doonesbury . . ."

February 2, 1984

"Hi Ronnie!"

March 9, 1984

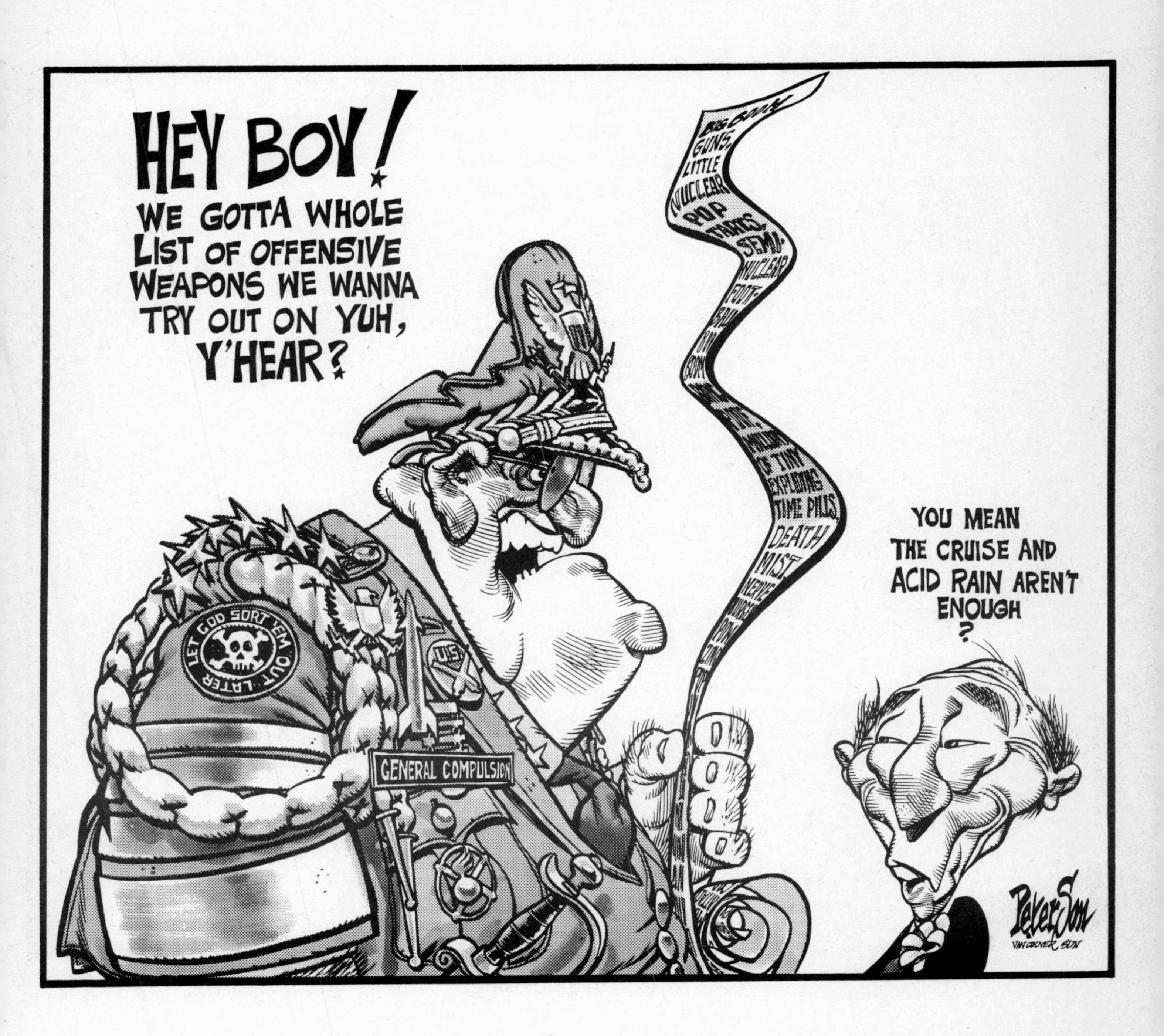
HEY BOY! WE GOTTA WHOLE LIST OF OFFENSIVE WEAPONS WE WANNA TRY OUT ON YUH, Y'HEAR?
GUNS,
LITTLE
NUCLEAR
POP
TARTS,
SEMI-
NUCLEAR
FOOT-
OF TINY
EXPLODING
TIME PILLS,
DEATH
MIST,
NERVE
LET GOD SORT 'EM OUT LATER
US
GENERAL COMPULSION
YOU MEAN THE CRUISE AND ACID RAIN AREN'T ENOUGH?
Peterson
VANCOUVER SUN

11

It's time to break up, all dreams must end

TERMINALLY COOL, Pierre Trudeau took leave of his office with elegance and grace, happy not to linger merely as macho proof of his longevity or self-importance. More than any of his predecessors, he had made tough, unpopular decisions and challenged the voters to like him or lump him. They did both. By the winter of 1984, Canada's political terrain had become either a graveyard (the West) or a minefield (the rest of the country), and the electorate was lying in wait to humble him.

In his novel *The Deer Park*, Norman Mailer described as a law of life that "one must grow, or else pay more for remaining the same." On that basis, Trudeau had overdrawn his psychic account. He decided to quit because he couldn't think of a good reason to stay. The constitution was home; bilingualism was permanently in place; his peace initiative was stalled; the economy seemed beyond salvation. There was no fun in the nation's business any more; half the provincial premiers were acting like reactionary duds and the Tory Opposition had a respectable leader who didn't provide much good sport.

Another disturbing element for this most introspective of prime ministers had been the cabinet shuffle in the summer of 1983. William Rompkey, a Newfoundland Liberal who had bountifully established his bumbling incompetence, was replaced as minister of Mines by a former high school principal from Burin-St. George's named Roger Simmons. Not only did a subsequent trial find Simmons guilty of tax evasion but his testimony revealed that he'd neglected to have his driving license renewed for so long that he was allowed to use his car only on a week-by-week basis; that his life insurance was cancelled because he forgot to pay the premiums; that he seemed to have overlooked the fact that he had teeth, because when he finally got to a dentist he had ten cavities and three rotting molars. To replace this simple Simmons, Trudeau re-appointed Bill Rompkey, but the experience left him shaken and muttering about bottoms of barrels.

Trudeau had always cast himself more as a moralist than as a survivor, and despite the avalanche of attacks on his policies and his person, by the winter of 1984, his ego did not feel particularly lacerated. Nor were his sensibilities exhausted or instincts blunted. Yet it was time to move on to a new phase of his life. Looking at what he had accomplished and at all the many things left to do, he must have felt a sense of weariness and disillusionment; the future seemed disordered and senseless. The essence of his mood was best caught in a fragment of dialogue from the film *Night Moves*. In it, Gene Hackman plays a private detective who loves watching the Washington Redskins on TV. At the movie's start, he is chipper, talking about football (and life) as a contest that can be won. But his optimism gradually evaporates and he concludes that life has become just like all those football games: "Nobody wins," he remarks to no one in particular. "One side just keeps losing slower than the other . . ."

Trudeau kept his blue mood private, except for one curious occasion in mid-October 1983 when he interrupted a political speech he was giving at Strathroy to deliver a soliloquy on his thoughts as he was being driven through the Ontario heartland, a soliloquy that spoke of his bewilderment at the country he administered, but never truly understood: "There was acre upon acre of farmland, and all we could see—though I pressed my forehead against the cold window—all we could see were little lights here and there. And I was wondering: what kind of people lived in those houses? And what kind of people lived, loved and worked in this part of Canada?"

At about this time, the public opinion polls, which had swung in a tidal wave of approval for the choice of Brian Mulroney as the freshly minted leader of the Progressive Conservative Party six months before, were failing to show any significant return to the Liberals. Not even the publicity surrounding Trudeau's peace initiative had budged his ratings very much. In Toronto, Mashel Teitelbaum, the artist who had circulated the original petition urging Trudeau to take up the Liberal leadership, was now sponsoring a very different appeal: "Since you seem to be totally out of touch with the everyday struggles of your constituents," he urged his former hero, "we, as your humble subjects, beseech you for the sake of the future of this country to do the honorable thing—and step down."

The Ottawa press corps was fretting to use all those prewritten resignation think-pieces and in-depth TV reports. On the evening of February 28, Trudeau phoned Martin Goldfarb, the Liberal Party's guru on public opinion. The good news was that Liberal fortunes had at last started to climb, with the party as popular as it had been in the 1980 election; the bad news was that even though Trudeau was never more highly respected, most voters felt strongly that it was time for him to go.

The prime minister walked out into Ottawa's worst blizzard in four years, thought over his options and decided to resign. "I went out to see if there were any signs of my destiny in the sky," he said the next morning, "but there weren't—there was nothing but snowflakes."

The initial reaction was unexpectedly muted. Some obvious Trudeau-haters, such as the *Toronto Sun*'s Peter Worthington, declared that he wanted "to drive a wooden stake through Trudeau's heart" to make sure he was really finished. Most commentators, however, agreed with Trudeau's blood enemy, Réné Lévesque, who remarked: "He sure made things more interesting—not necessarily more appealing, but certainly more interesting."

And so the Trudeau Years ended with the country moving toward yet another general election, still digging for its soul. The proposition Professor Kenneth McNaught, the University of Toronto historian, had put forth when Trudeau first joined the Liberal Party ("His commitment is an act of supreme symbolic importance, and his political fate will likely be the political fate of Canada . . .") had yet to be proved or disproved. When I asked McNaught to reflect on his forecast, he replied: "I'm not surprised to see how accurately I predicted things. The great issues in Canada are the federal-provincial structure, language and religion, and these were the areas for which Trudeau went into politics and had his greatest success. He can legitimately say, 'I've done what had to be done.' Without his victory in 1968, Canada would not have been recognizable today."

That was true enough. Pierre Trudeau, the most inspiring and most reviled prime minister this country has ever elected, had saved Canada. And the reason most Canadians were so ambivalent about the man was that they remained ambivalent about their country. We were glad to have him as a visitor in our time—and a lot gladder he was moving on.

Trudeau had already issued his own best epitaph years before. In a television interview on January 1, 1969, he said: "I'm quite prepared to die politically, when the people think I should. You know, politicians should be like Trappists who go around in monasteries, and the only words they can say to each other are: 'Brother, we must die one day.' I think this is true of politicians. Brother, someday we may be beaten. If I am, what will I do? The world is so full of a number of things, I'm sure we could all be as happy as kings."

During the intervening decade and a half, Pierre Elliott Trudeau, the constitutional lawyer turned prime minister, had broadened his universe and made the world his stage. No matter which theatre he chooses to occupy next, he will continue to uphold his ultimate civil liberty: the right to be himself.

12

The long goodbye

He came, conquered, quit and reconsidered and when he finally went, it was first class all the way.

November 16, 1979

The Boogie Man

March 5, 1980

October 29, 1981

"No firm offers yet from the UN or the North-South nations . . . however, there is an opening at quarterback with the Toronto Argonauts . . . "

August 26, 1982

November 10, 1982

"See! Over there! Looming large on the horizon . . . it looks like . . . yes, yes, once again . . . John Turner!"

August 31, 1983

". . . forget the Mulroney win — read that news item again where the Israeli cabinet implored Begin not to resign . . ."

September 14, 1983

Mr. T

September 15, 1983

"As you know, we've tightened up our security checks on cabinet post applications . . . you weren't attracted by the tax-free aspects of the job, were you. . . ?"

September 16, 1983

"Fortunately the future of mankind is safe. We were able to trap The Last Conservative Leader Extant on our first attempt. . . ."

February 8, 1984

". . . nice, Pierre, nice . . . now can we get a shot of you unfolding outside the universe . . ."

February 29, 1984

Sigh

March 1, 1984

"I'd like to thank the prime minister for responding to Opposition requests and opening up the special employment initiative program to all political parties . . . beginning with his own job. . . ."

March 2, 1984

". . . driven sparingly and only between Winnipeg and Montreal . . . runs on a deficit . . . make an offer — any offer . . . "

February 4, 1980

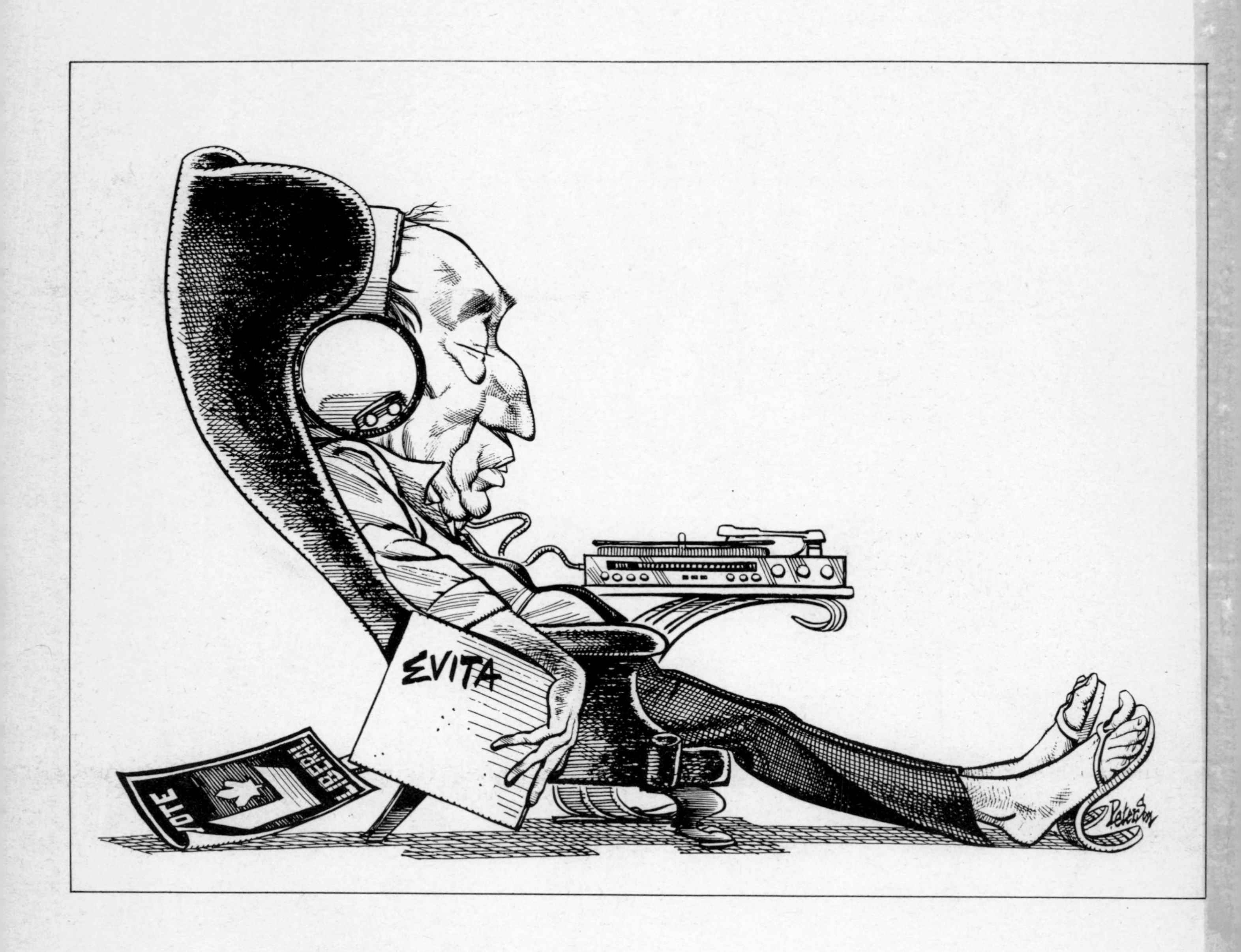